ROYAL WINTON PORCELAIN
CERAMICS FIT FOR A KING

Eileen Rose Busby

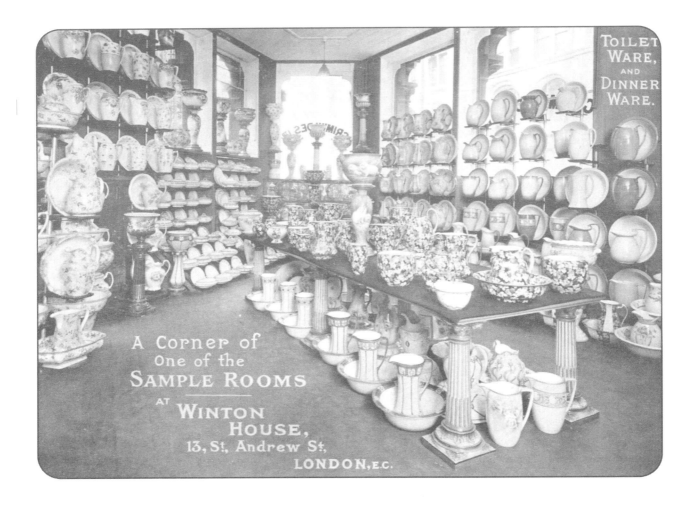

TOILET WARE, AND DINNER WARE.

A Corner of One of the SAMPLE ROOMS AT WINTON HOUSE, 13, St, Andrew St, LONDON, E.C.

Dedication

To all my kids with love—to Cordelia, who introduced me to Royal Winton; and to Cathy, Sally, Michael and Jon, for their unfailing encouragement and support. Also to my husband, Richard, my partner in the never-ending search for Grimwade/Royal Winton, who made it fun.

ACKNOWLEDGMENTS

Many thanks to the friends and dealers in various parts of the United States, Canada and England for their help in our search for Royal Winton ware.

Thanks to Reg Bladen for locating information about Grimwade/Royal Winton, especially for providing the model pot bank and the 1913 catalog. Thanks to both Reg and May Bladen for sharing their memories of what it was like to grow up in the Potteries.

Dealers and friends Frances and Brian Rothery, shared their knowledge and located special pieces for us in their part of England.

Thanks to Richard's cousin John, and his wife Valerie, for putting us up and for putting up with us on our many trips to Kent, England visiting antique shows and shops.

To our friends and neighbors in the little Suffolk village of Coney Weston, who taught us more than they realize about all things British: thanks for the memories and the good times.

And finally, thanks go to David Richardson, my publisher, who made it all possible. To all of you who have helped so much, my heartfelt thanks.

Grimwade wares on display at the King's Hall, Stoke-on-Trent, during the Potteries Exhibition. This selection was inspected by King George V and Queen Mary on their 1913 visit to the Potteries.

TABLE OF CONTENTS

LIFE IN THE POTTERIES

Staffordshire, England is a district long renowned for its ceramic production.* Since the 18th century, it has been—and continues to be—the heart and home of English china and earthenware production. But the ceramic industry actually began there centuries earlier.

Excavations indicate that pottery was being made in Staffordshire before the Roman occupation in AD 43. Fragments of pottery dating back to Neolithic times (c. 2500–1900 BC) have been found, as well as more "modern" Roman and Saxon pieces. Fourteenth-century kilns found in Stoke-on-Trent were fired with local coal.

One of the earliest known potters was Josiah Wedgewood, who set up shop in Staffordshire in 1759, followed by others factories such as Copeland, Spode, Minton and Doulton, all of which are still in business. Today, Staffordshire continues to be a name synonymous with the production of fine chinaware and pottery.

In the 17th century, pottery production consisted mostly of plain, utilitarian earthenware items, with special occasion pieces made to commemorate coronations, birthdays, weddings or other noteworthy events in the Royal family. This changed in 1657 with the introduction to England of a new beverage from China, called tea. A popular custom among the wealthy (who could afford to buy the precious and expensive leaves), tea drinking created a new market and a need for high-quality ceramic ware.

Wooden tea caddies were created, with locks to protect against thievery, as well as teapots, cups and saucers to store, infuse and drink the tasty beverage. Taking the place of ale as a regular breakfast drink, this new and pleasurable practice spread until the entire country became a nation of tea drinkers. Tea drinking was also popular among American settlers, becoming a key part of the country's history with the 1773 Boston Tea Party, an uprising protesting England's tax on the imported drink.

With the availability of less expensive tea leaves, tea drinking was no longer limited to the wealthy, and the custom spread until today tea is the world's most popular beverage. An estimated one billion cups a day are consumed worldwide, according to Elin McCoy's article "Tea, It's Just the Cure" (*Reader's Digest*, June 1997). This was, of course, a boon to pottery makers since it further increased the market for tea sets.

During its heyday, Staffordshire, England—with over 400 pottery factories located within a 10-mile radius—became known as "The Potteries." It was the heart and home of England's pottery industry, and the ideal place for pottery-making since there were ample supplies of clay, coal and water close at hand.

Nearby waterways provided sea transportation for export to the European and North American

Replica of a "pot bank." Early pottery factories, whether large or small, were called "pot banks." They were completely furnished with equipment from the clay to firing stages, and included the potter's living quarters. Courtesy of Reg Bladen.

---

* Ceramics: Greek, Keramikes; French, Keramos; potters clay, pottery. Of or relating to manufacturing of any product such as earthenware, brick, porcelain, or vitreous enamel, made from a non-metallic material by firing at high temperature. (From *Webster's New Collegiate Dictionary*)

A young worker in the plate-making shop
at Grimwades, Stoke-on-Trent.

"The whole area was built like one big factory," said Reg in an interview. "As you walked along the road, each opening was a different pottery. Nearly all the employment revolved around 'The Potteries.' It was either that or the coal mines for the boys. The girls could work in the shops or as decorators in the potteries."

"Watching the painters was ever so fascinating," May told us, smiling at the memory. "Some pieces had a transfer motif in the middle and were painted 'round the edges. With others, the conveyor belt moved pieces past, and the painters would add a dab of green for the leaves. They put such a lot of paint on their brushes that it looked as though it would fall off and ruin the piece, but only a bit came off."

An early account of the life of a potter paints a dreary picture. In *Sketches of Pottery Life and Character*, author T. Hawley writes: "In the mid-1900s the life span of a potter was only 35 years. After a lifetime of working in the constant smoke and soot, they often contracted 'potter's rot,' a disease of the lungs. Children as young as eight customarily

continents, Australia and New Zealand. The advent of the railroad added yet another way for Potteries to ship their wares, and for vacationers and commercial buyers to visit the area. In the 19th century, all industry in the area revolved around the Potteries, or "pot banks." It was not an uncommon practice for children as young as eight years to be employed there.

The pottery making process began with a modeling department, the group of workers responsible for molding or shaping the wares. Ceramic pieces underwent an initial firing, after which time they were decorated, painted or enameled, and fired again. A finishing glaze was then applied to the piece before a final firing. Hot kilns and soot from the many furnaces were landmark to these large factories.

A latecomer to the scene near the end of the 19th century, the Grimwade/Royal Winton factory would be recognized and respected for the variety, beauty and quality of its wares. When Richard and I were searching England for publications on Grimwade/Royal Winton, a London magazine seller referred us to Reg Bladen who deals in rare, antiquarian and second-hand books, and whose specialty is ceramics and pottery. Reg and his wife, May, both grew up in the Potteries and remember it well.

Sketch of village life, and pot banks during firing. From the cover of an early booklet entitled *Sketches of Pottery Life and Character* by T. Hawley, c. 1906.

Above: Modelers work in the mould shop at Grimwades.

Below: Decorators in the gilding and enameling department.

worked long hours for little pay." Much has been said about the fact that young girls worked in the Potteries and were paid only pennies for their labor. Child labor was an accepted practice, and wages were comparable with the times. While we can be thankful this no longer occurs in our society, we cannot change the past.

The pure, pristine appearance of the finished wares seemed a paradox as May Bladen shared with us her vivid childhood memories of the dirty, coal-fired kilns at work. "On the way home from school all the kilns were burning. It seemed as though they only fired when it was time for school to let out. Everywhere was like a black fog. By the time I got home, my face and dress were black with soot. I remember my mother washing the floors every day, and the curtains every week. The step-stones outside the door were filthy dirty every morning and had to be scrubbed. It was something we were used to, part of life in the potteries."

Reg mentioned the time he worked at a gentlemen's outfitter. "We wore white removable collars. I carried two parcels to work—one held lunch, and the other a spare collar. By lunchtime, our collars were black, and had to be changed."

He recalled that even Leonard Grimwade himself (co-founder of Grimwade Brothers/Royal Winton Pottery) recognized the unhealthful aspects of life in the factories. "Our families all worked in the potteries. I was eight or nine in the early 1930s. As a special Sunday treat through the church, we were brought to what we called "Grimwades Bungalows." This was to get the children out of the potteries for a bit of fresh air, and to get away for a time from the constant smoke. We were given a bag of buns and a drink."

From its beginnings in 1885, Grimwade Brothers (later to become Royal Winton) had been a leading pottery manufacturer, its common wares turning up in all households, including the Royal household. It wasn't until 100 years later that Royal Winton finally received its due recognition for decorative pieces, beginning in the mid-1990s with the "re-discovery" of highly collectible transfer-ware chintz . While Royal Winton chintz remains eagerly sought after by collectors, this book will also describe and illustrate the vast number of other wares made by the company over the years.

CHAPTER ONE

ROYAL WINTON
HOW IT GREW AND PROSPERED

Royal Winton had its beginnings in the young Grimwade Brothers firm, founded in 1885 in Stoke-on-Trent, Staffordshire, England. In the Grimwade family today, Leonard's descendants say that he started the business and his brothers Edward and Sidney joined him later. Sidney's family states that he began the pottery and Leonard joined him later. However the firm began, no one disputes the fact that it was Leonard who carried it on.

Leonard Grimwade (1863–1931) had both an inventive streak and an entrepreneurial flair. Born in Ipswich, a town in Suffolk County, England, Leonard began his business life with his uncle as a dry salter in the Potteries. He came to the Potteries as a young man to work as a modeler, but quickly moved to manufacturing.

In 1885–6, Leonard and his brothers—Edward Ernest and Sidney Richard—purchased a shed between two rows of cottages and began pottery operations there as Grimwade Brothers (also called Winton Pottery). Leonard worked as a pottery decorator and modeler, while Sidney was primarily a potter. Edward would later move to New Zealand and represent the company's interests there. The range of wares Grimwade Brothers made over the years was vast, beginning with plain and practical everyday items, and moving into more beautiful and decorative pieces.

Leonard was a key factor in the company's growth, recognizing the value of new ideas, changing economy and improved methods. An innovator who patented many things over the years, his involvement resulted in a variety of designs and wares which he varied to suit what he perceived to be the public need or demand.

By 1887, larger quarters were needed and the entire factory moved into a new location, the Winton Hotel in Stoke-on-Trent, which featured showrooms for visiting buyers. Sales doubled every year, and in 1890 an export department was established, along with a London showroom at Ely Place in Holborn, England.

In 1892, a new four-story Winton factory was built on the main road of Stoke-on-Trent, only a three minute walk from the railroad station. The property had an impressive 180-foot frontage and covered two acres.

Grimwade Brothers expanded again in 1900 with the acquisition of Winton Pottery Co., Ltd., and Stoke Pottery, the latter owned by Mr. James Plant, Sr. A profitable find, the Stoke plant had a large range of ovens and kilns, plus complete milling materials such as flint and Cornish stone,

Leonard Lumsden Grimwade
1863–1931

A panoramic view of one of the warehouses at Winton Pottery, displaying some of the Grimwade toilet and household wares.

James Plant, Sr. and T. Watkin, Directors

and was conveniently located adjacent to the Trent and Mersey Canals.

The three Potteries—Grimwade Bros., Winton Pottery and Stoke Pottery—combined under the new name Grimwades Limited. Leonard became Chairman and Managing Director; Sidney, Edward, James Plant and T. Watkin served as Directors. The London showroom moved to larger quarters on St. Andrews Street, and has since been known as "Winton House."

Edward and Sidney retired from the Board of Directors in 1900, leaving Leonard Grimwade, James Plant, Sr. and T. Watkin as the firm's sole Directors.

In 1901, under Leonard Grimwade's initiative, Grimwades Limited inaugurated new methods of kiln and enamel firing, using the Climax and Rotary kilns, in which a number of pieces could be packed into iron cages on wheels, and pulled in and out of the furnace mechanically. By allowing more pottery to be fired at once, and offering a means of temperature control, the new kilns increased fuel economy, and provided more lustrous color and more brilliant gold.

Later that same year, Queen Victoria died and was succeeded by her son, King Edward VII. In preparation for Edward's 1902 coronation, the Grimwades plants hummed with activity, operating kilns day and night to produce half-a-million souvenir pieces in a few short weeks. Just before the coronation date, two disastrous fires—one at Stoke Pottery and the other at Winton Pottery—destroyed 80,000 souvenir pieces that had been ready for delivery. Tremendous effort and round-the-clock firing resulted in all of the destroyed pieces being replaced and delivered on time, literally hot from the fires.

The Grimwades expansion continued into 1906–7, with the acquisition of four more Potteries: Rubian Art Pottery; Upper Hanley Pottery; Atlas China of Stoke; and Heron Cross Pottery of Fenton. When the other companies were acquired, their names sometimes appeared on backstamps of

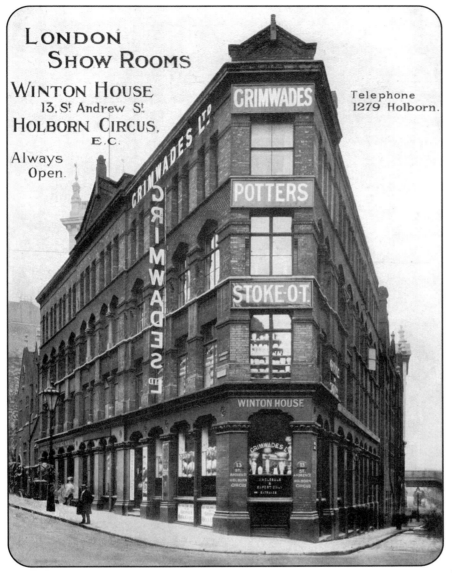

The London showroom on St. Andrews Street after 1900,
familiarly called "Winton House."

the Chrome Transfer and Potters Supply Company, which provided chrome and lithographic transfers, ceramic colors, potters' materials and other products needed to produce the transfer ware the company was now making in volume.

In association with Brittain's of Cheddleton (perhaps a paper manufacturer), Leonard devised a thin printing tissue with a detachable backing, known as "Duplex" paper, which facilitated the handling of lithographic sheets, helping to make the lithographic process commercially viable. This process involved printing a design on the thin tissue (or Duplex paper), gluing the paper onto the ceramic, and letting it dry. When the paper was later removed with a sponge and hot water, the design was permanently affixed (or transferred) onto the piece. This process was similar to the way we apply decals today, although not quite as easy.

Much of the company's transfer ware was embellished with gold trim or enameling. More than just an embellishment, enameling was sometimes used as a decorative method for camouflaging imperfections in a piece.

each piece. The addition of these firms, with their many ovens and kilns, allowed Grimwades Ltd. to produce quality china tea sets at moderate prices.

Soon, the company was known as a major manufacturer of chinaware and earthenware toilet articles. They proudly declared themselves to be one of the best equipped factories in the world. Their foreign trade grew, with overseas agents in Canada, Australia, New Zealand, India, Germany, South Africa, Sweden, Norway and the United States.

Sanitation was a major concern in these days before widespread refrigeration, and Grimwades Ltd. attempted to address the problem. In 1908, the firm began obtaining patents on "Hygienic Pottery" for home and hospital use. Leonard bought shares in

Always ahead of his time, Leonard consistently sought ideas for new products, and ways to improve quality and efficiency while increasing profits. His son, Charles Donavan, had been head of a tile and and brickworks company in China, testing new methods and materials overseas. This no doubt inspired Leonard Grimwade in his efforts, as well as provided the inspiration for some of the company's Oriental patterns, acclaimed for their variety of color and design.

When King Edward VII died in 1910 after a short reign, the Grimwades Ltd. again had occasion to work at full speed. An article in *The Glass and China Trader* dated 1910 stated that Grimwades produced 850,000 souvenir mugs and beakers in five weeks' time for the coronation of King George V and Queen Mary in 1911. (Of these, 500,000

Advertisement appearing in *The Glass and China Trader*, December 1912, for the new Grimwades "Quick-Cooker" Bowl.

were made at the Winton Pottery factory alone.)

Patents were issued for the Quick-Cooker, Fly-less Milk Bowl, Hygienic Jug, Bevel Edge Drainer, Pie Dish with air vents, an oval household jar, Perfection Pie Funnel and others. Hygienic pottery continued to be popular, with enthusiastic descriptions and instructions printed directly on some of the wares, such as "The most comfortable and sanitary bedpan in the world." These domestic items were made without corners or angles, designed for easier cleaning and to make household chores more sanitary. The Grimwade Quick-Cooker was certified by the Institute of Hygiene, and awarded a gold medal at the 1911 Festival of Empire Imperial Exhibition.

In 1913, realizing that merchandise display was becoming crucial to marketing, Grimwades Limited applied for patent rights for their Rotary Display stands. These were steel stands with stained wooden shelves, built to hold 12 half tea sets (consisting of a teapot, four cups and four saucers), 12 covered dishes and plates, or 12 ewers and basins.

The company also obtained patents for its "Ideal" Display Blocks and wires, designed to show whole sets of jugs, teacups and saucers, teapots, butter dishes and blancmange molds. Smaller blocks were used for display of trios (cup, saucer and small tea plate) and dinnerware. Previous displays had been limited to shelves, so the blocks were an attractive improvement.

A later advertisement for the patented "Ideal" Display Stand.

The Glass and China Trader published an article in January 1913, describing and extolling the virtues of Grimwades' Ideal Display Stand, innovative for the times.

1913 turned out to be a banner year, with a Royal visit made to the Winton Potteries by King George V and Queen Mary. On April 22, the factory's potters stood out front of the building, each holding a banner with one letter. Together, the banners spelled their motto: "No craft there is that can with ours compare. We make our pots of what we potters are."

To Leonard Grimwade's delight, the Queen admired the Quick-Cooker and a Mecca Foot Warmer in the Jacobean pattern (a vine-leafed chintz design based on a 9th century tapestry), and both items were proudly presented to her as a gift during her visit.

Never shy about promoting his wares, Leonard made sure the public knew about this great honor by featuring the Royal visit in a company catalog printed shortly afterward. This 1913 catalog featured a brief history of the firm, press notices concerning the Royal visit, photographs of various salesrooms and factories, a list of Board members at the time, and color illustrations of products displayed on Atlas Rotary Stands. One advertisement listed the company name as "Royal Winton," no doubt inspired by the occasion. Although there is no record that formal permission was granted to use that name, the Royal Winton title grew on the firm.

A coal strike that year could have brought production to a halt had it not been for the firm's Climax kiln, requiring less coal and ensuring mass production of wares.

By the first World War, the five Grimwades plants had employed over 1,000 workers, and in 1920, Charles Donavan Grimwade was put in charge of a new laboratory for the purpose of improving quality, methods and materials, aimed at making the company more competitive. His previous experience with the tile and brickworks company in China proved to be an asset to the firm. Grimwades pioneered long, gas-fired tunnel ovens, capable of turning out as much as six full-size ovens, providing mass production of its fine wares.

The railroad strike of 1921 turned out to be a blessing in disguise, as it inspired Leonard Grimwade to buy a "Karrier" or motor lorry (delivery van) for making customer deliveries. Grimwades Ltd. also began transporting their own wares via waterways and canals, boasting "no breakage—no delay—no incivility on the part of carriers, and a lessening of serious inconveniences." The

King George V and Queen Mary as pictured in the Grimwades 1913 Catalog commemorating the Royal Visit.

transport was successful for providing faster and less expensive delivery.

By 1928, the name "Royal Winton" began to regularly appear in company advertising and catalogs. A third showroom—called the Victorian Showroom—was opened at Winton House in Stoke-on-Trent. Each one was different. The Royal Showroom at Winton House displayed dinnerware, teapots, coffee pots, and toilet ware. The new Victorian Showroom was used to display tableware, bowls, vases and jardinieres, while the Excelsior Showroom at Winton House held clearance sale items only.

In the 1930s, Royal Winton began producing a number of kinds of chintz and relief ware, offering a wide range of designs. A year later, the firm underwent some change when Leonard was killed in a road accident on January 26, 1931. The following obituary appeared in the March 2, 1931 edition of *Pottery Gazette*:

Leonard Lumsden Grimwade was born in Ipswich about 1863, the son of Richard Grimwade. . . . A Liberal free-trader, [Leonard] was elected to Stoke upon Trent council and was also appointed to the local magistrate's bench. He was secretary of the Potteries Association for the Promotion of Federation, founded in 1907, and published 160 favourable replies to a circular letter to leaders of trade and industry in his Book of Opinions. Questioned by counsel for Fenton during the passage of the federation bill through Parliament and asked where he lived, he replied "I sleep in Wolstanton, but I live at the Potteries." He unsuccessfully contested the parliamentary election in Hanley as a Liberal in 1918. He was a member of King Street, Newcastle, Congregational Church.

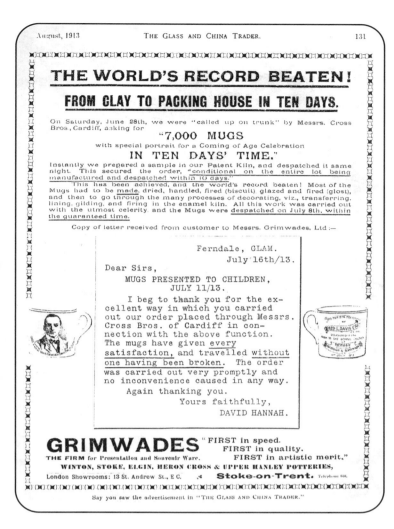

Grimwade modified his free-trade views to some extent during the First World War, by which time his five factories employed 1,000 people. In December 1917 he printed a message from the prime minister asking for economy in consumption of food on reduced sized butter dishes, milk jugs and plates, which sold at one shilling each.

He married twice and had two sons and two daughters. His first wife, Marion, was elected to the Stoke Board of Guardians in 1897. Leonard Lumsden Grimwade was killed in a road accident on 26 January, 1931 and was buried in Hartshill cemetery.

James Plant, Sr. also died in 1931, leaving James Plant, Jr. as Managing Director of the firm, a position he held until 1962. During James Jr.'s years as Managing Director, production continued as usual, with new additions of chintz designs; lustre, pastel,

commemorative and souvenir ware; and handpainted pieces signed by the artist.

Following the death of King George V in 1936, Grimwades Ltd. produced hundreds of thousands of commemorative pieces in anticipation of the coronation of King Edward VIII, who promptly abdicated the throne. New items were then made to honor his brother, crowned King George VI that same year. Soon after George's death in 1953, his daughter Elizabeth was crowned Queen, resulting in another occasion for Royal Winton commemorative wares.

James Jr. died in 1964, marking the end of Royal Winton's "golden years" under the direction of the Grimwade and Plant families. The Howard Pottery Co. Ltd. took over the firm, retaining the Royal Winton name and continuing production. Since then, there have been other owners but the firm has remained Royal Winton, producing tableware, giftware and recently reissuing limited editions of early chintz patterns.

It is interesting to note the great attention that Royal Winton had given to its record keeping. According to *The Glass and China Trader* from October 1913, Grimwades was "a business that ranks now as one of the largest in the Potteries. . . . A dozen typewriters are kept constantly at work, and the complete system of filing all correspondence and orders makes it possible to successfully cope with the immense detail work of this huge business." Unfortunately, most company records were either lost or destroyed. But old catalogs, press notices, advertisements and magazine articles still survive, containing information about the firm.

Today, Royal Winton has come nearly full circle with the revival of their most famous product, chintz. Other companies have followed suit. In 1997, the firm introduced the first in a series of limited edition reproductions of some of their most popular chintz patterns from the 1930s, with an 11" vase in the Florence pattern.

From its small beginnings, Royal Winton grew into a highly productive and well respected Pottery known for the innovative beauty and perfection of its wares. Ceramics from Royal Winton's golden years (early 1900s to the 1960s) continue to be the most sought after and treasured today.

CHAPTER TWO

WHAT THE COMPANY PRODUCED

In their early years (1886 to 1913) Grimwades' mainstay production consisted of toilet wares, household wares, nursery items and other "cottage comforts" as they were called. The variety of items necessary to keep an efficient household was nothing short of amazing, and Royal Winton produced a vast number of wares for every use and occasion.

The following is a comprehensive list of what they produced: baskets, beakers, bed pans, bed pots, biscuit barrels, bonbon dishes, bowls, boxes (musical, candy, trinket), breakfast/bedside sets, cake plates on pedestals, cake stands, candlesticks, celery trays, chamber pots, chamber sticks, character and drinking mugs, cheese keepers, coffee and hot water pots, clocks, covered butter dishes, compotes, creamers, cruets/condiment sets, cups and saucers, dinnerware, egg cups, foot warmers, honey pots, humidors, inhalers, jam/marmalade pots, jardinieres, jelly molds, jugs, lamp bases, lemon squeezers, mint/sauce boats on trays, mustard pots, nut dishes, pie bakers, pie birds, pin trays, plates, pudding basins, relish dishes, salt/pepper shakers, sandwich trays, sardine dishes (rare), snack sets, sugar shakers, sweets dishes, tea sets, teapots (2, 4 or 6 cup capacity), toast racks (2 or 4 slice), toilet sets, trivets, vases and wall pockets.

While the shapes and variations of their items were many, Royal Winton boasted rich and vibrant colors such as the pink, yellow, green and cream used in their pastel line; and the deeper orange, green, brown and reds used in their cottage ware.

A 1913 press notice from the *Daily Mail* newspaper correctly stated that "Winton pottery is produced in practically every form to meet the requirements of the table or household, whether for use or ornamental." The firm's semi-porcelain ware was mainly intended for the working class, while the carriage trade (or upper class) preferred finer and more delicate bone china. However, even the upper classes needed everyday household items, which Grimwades produced in volume. To suit the finer taste, most Royal Winton pieces were thinner and lighter in weight than other Potteries', making them easily distinguishable.

Some pieces had special traits. Many of the salt and pepper shakers, creamers and sugars, mint boats, bedside sets, condiment and cruet sets had matching trays with indentations to fit each item. Cups for bedside sets varied according to the buyer's choice. Covered butters were rectangular or square in shape, while covered muffin dishes were generally round.

Royal Winton advertised 20 different shapes of cheese keepers, in several sizes, all higher at one end

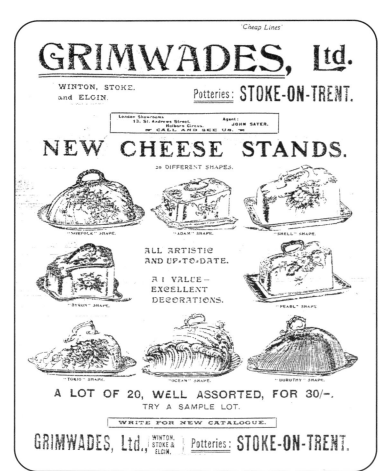

Grimwades proudly offered 20 different Cheese Stands, shown in this 1905 advertisement from *The Glass and China Trader*. The assortment was called "a very popular Edwardian 'cheap line.'"

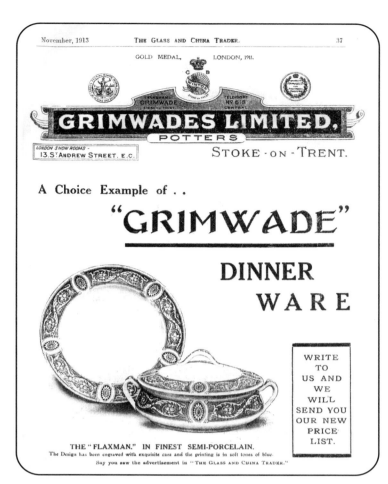

Advertisement for Grimwades' semi-porcelain dinnerware that appeared in *The Glass and China Trader*, November 1913. Grimwade/Royal Winton excelled in their Transfer Ware.

to accommodate a wedge of cheese. The cover on the keeper had a finger loop rather than a knob.

Egg cups were single or double capacity, designed to hold hen and duck eggs. The same blanks, alike in shape and size, were often decorated in various ways: with pastel colors, chintz patterns, lustre or mottled effect, Rosebud, souvenir or handpainted.

Vases came in various heights and shapes, designed to hold single buds or bunches of flowers; toast racks typically held two or four slices of bread (3 or 5 bar). Cruet and bedside sets were popular on both continents, but the stacking teapot was most popular with Americans.

In a glowing account of Leonard Grimwade and the company's progress, *The Glass and China Trader* in 1913 stated that "Grimwades Ltd. brought out no less than 1,726 different toilet shapes, earning for the firm the reputation of having the largest range of toilet sets in the world."

TIMELINE OF PRODUCTION

Practical household items were the firm's bread and butter in the early years (1886–1910). Mundane but necessary items such as wash stands and jugs, chamber pots, tableware, dinnerware and other patented pieces found their way into most households, collectively described as "housewifely conveniences that make for cottage comfort." Some were undecorated, but most had floral designs of some sort. Transfer ware—pieces created by transferring a design from Duplex paper to the ceramic—was intended for hall, study and boudoir use. Two of the earliest all-over transfer patterns were Spode and Hampton.

During World War I (1913–1918), austerity became the order of the day. Grimwades' output was necessarily curtailed, especially of the highly decorated pieces, resulting in their plain white utility ware.

In the 1920s, while Europe was recovering from the war, Grimwades introduced art and novelty pieces. King Tutankhamen's tomb was unearthed in 1922, an internationally significant event that caused some Grimwade patterns to show an Egyptian influence.

A good variety of lustre ware was produced between the 1920s and 1940s, including Byzanta, Golden Age (offering the same metallic look as gold) and Silver Age (offering the same metallic look as silver). Lustre was a term that applied to pottery covered with an iridescent metallic film or glaze, which was fired on.

In 1928, Royal Winton began making its chintz ware in dozens of patterns with closely packed floral designs. Chintz could be found on jardinieres, vases, toilet wares, and all sorts of tea and table services. Bedside sets—consisting of a tray with indentations to hold a toast rack, creamer, sugar, teapot and cup—and cottage ware became popular, comprising what most households used on a daily basis.

Relief ware was also introduced in 1928 and manufactured well into the 1940s. High-relief ware was defined by its lumpy, bumpy surface; while bas-relief ware simply had a design raised slightly above the surface of each piece.

In 1936, Royal Winton made thousands of commemorative items in anticipation of Edward VIII's coronation, and shortly afterward for the coronation of his brother, George VI. These pieces were produced in such large numbers that, in spite of Edward's abdicating the throne, many are still available today. A variety of floral aids, such as perching birds and flower arranging frogs, also made their appearance at this time.

The 1940s brought Rosebud ware—items with rosebuds and other small flowers done in relief on the handles, spouts and finials. Character mugs came on the market, depicting wartime heroes and leaders. These mugs are in demand today because of their limited production over a brief period of time.

Royal Winton's souvenir ware was introduced in the 1940s and '50s. These handpainted items appealed to travelers to England, Canada and the United States, featuring scenic views of popular vacation spots such as Niagara Falls, Yosemite Park and Canadian destinations. The pieces are valued today for their historical depiction of early views with uncluttered skylines. A wide range of items shaped like maple leaves was introduced, probably for export to Canada, whose national symbol is the maple leaf.

TRADEMARKS AND BACKSTAMPS

A fair knowledge of trademarks and backstamps is necessary to date and identify authentic Winton from possible reproductions. Because of ordinances stated in import/export laws, it is generally thought anything marked "England" was made prior to 1914, while anything marked "Made in England" was made after that date. However, this only applies to items that were specifically made for export.

After an item's second firing, and before glazing, the company trademark was generally rubber stamped on the back or underside of the piece. Some especially small items, such as salt and pepper shakers, were only marked "England" or "Made in England." Other pieces have no markings at all, or may have had a paper sticker which did not survive time and wear.

Grimwades issued a variety of different marks. Geoffrey Godden's *Encyclopedia of British Pottery and Porcelain Marks* illustrates those used from 1885–1951, but there were many others.

Early backstamps used by Grimwade Brothers. The six-sided star dates from 1886 to 1900.
From Geoffrey Godden's *Encyclopedia of British Pottery and Porcelain Marks*.

Backstamps from the 1930s and forward. Many of these include the pattern names.
From Geoffrey Godden's *Encyclopedia of British Pottery and Porcelain Marks*.

Straight-line Royal Winton backstamps
used after 1951.

According to Godden, the circular Royal Winton mark was not used until circa 1930. Later pieces used small print in a straight line, rather than the familiar circle mark.

c. 1951+   c. 1934–50

Some reproductions carry the circular Royal Winton mark, along with a statement that they are reproductions. Others can be recognized by the addition of LTD under Grimwades, or the circle drawn around the mark. In this case, we are defining "reproductions" two ways: pieces made by the current Royal Winton factory to imitate their earlier wares; and copies made by other factories altogether, stamped to appear as if they came from Royal Winton.

1995

A Jon Roth backstamp is frequently found on souvenir pieces made for the United States. Jon Roth was an English distributor of Royal Winton wares in the 1950s.

Pattern names or series marks—such as "Byzanta Ware" or "Shakespeare Series"—were often printed directly on a piece.

An "A" appears below the trademark on pieces that were produced after 1945, indicating one of several meanings. It may have referred to the quality of the ware. Or, it may have been given to designate the purpose of the item—utilitarian, decorative, etc. The most logical explanation is that British Potteries were divided into groups after World War II, according to what they produced and categorized by letters of the alphabet. Royal Winton was in the "A" category.

Most Grimwade/Royal Winton pieces manufactured between 1885 and the 1960s were marked with a some kind of a stamp or, less commonly, with

These marks appeared on series pieces, such as Minton, Byzanta, Shakespeare and Dickens. Series backstamps were often featured on the underside of the piece with the name of the character or design, such as "Orlando" or "Ye Olde Inne" (shown below).

a paper label. Because of the number and variation of these trademarks, items can usually be dated accurately to within a few years. Some of the marks may have faded over time, but most are still discernable. A word of warning: be sure the piece you buy has an old backstamp, unless you intend to buy a reproduction piece. Reproductions are being made in increasing numbers, by companies other than Royal Winton.

We define authentic Grimwade/Royal Winton as any of their wares—household or chintz—manufactured from 1885 to the 1960s. This book is intended to show that the variety of Royal Winton pieces was seemingly endless, and that these pieces from the past are still as beautiful and useful today as they were a century ago.

CHAPTER THREE

ROYAL WINTON PATTERNS AND DESIGNS

Royal Winton produced items which were made and decorated in various ways. Cottage ware is uniquely shaped. Rosebud pieces are recognized by their relief floral designs. Lustre ware has a finish that speaks for itself. And chintz is in a group all its own. This chapter is dedicated to the description of Grimwade/Royal Winton wares made from 1885 through the 1950s.

BYZANTA WARE

Byzanta was a descriptive lustre (more of an effect than a pattern), probably named after the Byzantine Empire, considered the center of Eastern European culture during the Middle Ages, and known for Oriental luxuriance and splendor. Royal Winton produced Byzanta ware briefly in the 1920s, and again in the late 1930s. Byzanta ware included the Shakespeare and Dickens series (pieces illustrated with handpainted Shakespeare or Dickens characters), as well as pieces decorated with Egyptian scenes.

An interesting Art Deco cup with a silhouette couple is also part of the Byzanta line. Byzanta colors were rich, vibrant and lustrous, including blue, green, rust, orange, cream, rouge red and yellow. Some of the same colored pieces in Byzanta carried different backstamps, according to when they were made, but most of them indicated "Byzanta." Illustrated on page 33.

CHINTZ WARE

The English have long had a love affair with flowers of any kind. With the popularity of England's chintz, so, too have the Americans. Most proper English gardens have a rose or two, as is reflected in most chintz patterns.

Webster's New Collegiate Dictionary defines chintz as a glazed, brightly printed calico fabric from India, called "chintes." Inexpensive "chintes" cotton fabric, covered with images of trees, birds and flowers, was first shipped to England in the early 19th century on East India Company ships. It is from this term that we derive the word "chintzy," meaning gaudy or cheap.

The English loved the imported designs and before long, British textile printers were creating their own chintz. Potters picked up on the idea, transferring these flowery designs to dish ware. Soon, English tableware happily bloomed with brightly colored roses, birds and butterflies. The colorful china caught the public's fancy, becoming more and more popular and continuing into the 1960s.

It was inexpensive ware intended for everyday use and sold in common stores like Woolworth's. Today, chintz ware still blossoms in a rainbow of color on shelves, cupboards and tables. It is highly collectible on both sides of the Atlantic, albeit considerably more expensive than when it first appeared.

Chintz is characterized by designs placed on plain, cross-hatched, solid color with dotted pebbly, bubbly or leafy backgrounds. The inspiration for these patterns came from everywhere—garden flowers, fabrics, tapestries, embroideries. It seemed that every piece of china imaginable was covered with chintz. There were egg cups, covered butter and cheese dishes, bedside sets, tea sets, cruets, wall pockets, toast racks (especially difficult to cover), coffee pots, jugs, clocks, jam pots, mustard pots, etc. The list is endless. Jam and mustard pots had ceramic, chrome or silver-plated lids.

Designs were painstakingly hand-applied using a lithographic process. First, unglazed ceramic pieces were brushed with glue, or "size", and left to become tacky. Transfers (or thin tissue paper with an imprinted design) were then carefully cut to fit the item to be decorated, pressed into place, and allowed to dry. The tissue paper was rubbed off with hot water and a sponge, leaving only the design, and the piece was fired in a kiln. The process was similar to the way we place decals today, although not quite as simple. Pattern names, gilding and lithographer's marks were added to the piece between the first and second firings.

Fitting the paper patterns on pieces of pottery or china was a tedious process, much like applying wallpaper in close spaces. The goal of the transfer process was perfection, so no seams or obvious joins were allowed to show. Typically, the handles and spouts on Royal Winton wares were also chintz-covered, a time-consuming procedure that was not always the case with wares made by other Potteries.

Today, "chintz" is the generic name for ceramic ware covered in closely packed floral transfer patterns. Many patterns are so much the same that collectors (and dealers) have inadvertently "married up" a cup and saucer with no identifying backstamp, only to find they were not a true match. Many pattern names are marked somewhere on the back or bottom of a piece.

Potteries often vied for the public's business by creating new patterns, or by "borrowing" from the competition. Since chintz patterns weren't copyrighted, similar or identical designs were commonly made by many different firms.

There are dozens of chintz designs, many of them easily recognized and named after the predominant flower, such as Anemone, Delphinium, English Rose and Sweet Pea. Others may have a girl's name, such as Julia, Hazel, Marion, Sweet Nancy or even Queen Anne. Still others are named for a season—Springtime, Summertime—or a well-known place in Britain—Balmoral, Bedale. Some have enameling over the pattern, probably intended to cover the iron specks or impurities (part of the raw material used) left on the pieces.

This "cheap and cheerful" chintz, which originally sold for pennies at Woolworth's, is today an expensive collectible. Prices range from $50 per piece to the thousands of dollars. A complete dinner set in a prized pattern may bring $5,000 or more. The more popular the pattern, the higher the price, especially at an auction. However it is not always wise to offer a premium price for a pattern that is currently popular. As the public's fancy changes, so do prices. Neither is it wise to buy a particular pattern as an investment thinking the price may go even higher. Collectors should buy because they like the pattern, and not in expectation that it might be worth more in the future.

MIGRATION OF CHINTZ

A large amount of Royal Winton's production was exported to Canada in the 1950s. Luckily however, quantities of it came to the United States with the British who settled here, including British war brides of American servicemen. During World War II, production of chintz was curtailed along with other decorative wares. In the early 1950s, advertisements once again appeared for this cheery chintz ware. Chintz production slowed again and finally ceased in the 1960s, most likely because it required a time-consuming procedure that was no longer cost effective with rising wages.

A word to chintz collectors: do not throw away broken pieces. Repaired cups can be used for small flower arrangements and there is a thriving business in jewelry made from broken bits of chintz. Royal Winton chintz is today's collectible because it combines beauty, variety and durability, making it a collector's delight.

CHINTZ PATTERNS

For many chintz collectors, the colors in the design are what attract the eye, but not all chintz patterns are vividly colored. Some collectors define chintz as floral transfer patterns having five or more colors. But some designs have paler tints, attracting a different type of collector.

Royal Winton began making chintz in 1928, its early designs consisting of Victorian patterns (similar to wallpaper designs of the 1920s), such as large roses on a somber background. Designs from the 1930s tended to be smaller and more closely spaced. Some floral designs were more fanciful than the ones for which they were named.

Backgrounds vary from solid to leafy, to cross-hatched to dotted. Most floral designs are variations of bouquets from an English garden. The following is an alphabetical listing of Royal Winton's chintz patterns, with a description. There may be other patterns than those listed, since "new" chintz continues to turn up. The origin of a name is stated if known.

ANEMONE (named after the flower) has two colorings: orange-centered creamy anemones on dark blue; or red-centered yellow anemones on a light blue background.

BALMORAL, named after Scotland's Royal castle, is a mixed bouquet of floral sprays on black.

BEDALE is named for a 14th century Yorkshire town. It has pink anemones, yellow daisies, and mixed floral sprays on a white background.

BEESTON, named for several British towns, has a black background in dramatic contrast to pink and yellow roses with small green leaves.

BIRDS AND TULIPS consists of a white background with blue polka dots, and the pieces are gilt-edged.

BLUE JADE consists of a few flowers (mostly in shades of blue) and pink roses, on a blue and white background.

BLUE TULIP has deep blue tulips, and pink and yellow flowers on a black background.

CARNATION pieces made for Australia were marked OSTRIA. This is a dramatic, widely spaced design with large red carnations on a deep blue background.

CHEADLE was probably named for a market town in the Staffordshire Hills. It is a colorful floral design in yellows, pinks and blues, with green leaves on a light background.

CHELSEA was named after a London area that served as a favorite haunt to artists and writers such as James McNeill Whistler and Oscar Wilde. It has large pink roses, small white and yellow flowers, and blue buds on a black background.

CHINTZ is another fanciful pattern, with large rose-colored anemones on a leafy green or blue background.

CLEVEDON was named after a small seaside resort on the coast of England. This design is sprinkled with green leaves, pink and yellow roses, and smaller blue and white flowers on a yellow dotted background. Pieces are edged in deep pink.

CLOISONNE consists of gold leaf tracings. Some pieces have small, enameled daisy-like white, yellow and blue enameled flowers, with red centers. The design rests on a green or cream background. Some pieces are marked "Royal Winton," others simply say "Cloisonne." W. R. Midwinter Ltd. made what appears to be an identical pattern.

CLYDE was named after the River Clyde which runs through Scotland. It features pale pastels with a color choice: apricot and yellow flowers with green leaves; or dark pink and yellow flowers with brown leaves, both on a white background. It has also been found as a study in blue.

COTSWOLD was named after the range of hills known as the center of England's timber industry. A less closely packed design, it is a pretty pattern with apple blossom buds, harebells and pink roses on white.

CRANSTONE, like Clevedon, shows sprouting green leaves, pink and yellow roses, and smaller blue and white flowers, but on a green dotted background.

CROCUS consists of yellow and blue crocuses, along with blue and pink sprigs of flowers on a black or white background. The two variations do not look alike at first glance because of the difference in backgrounds and patterns. It can also be found in black and white only.

CROMER was named for a holiday resort town in Norfolk, England. It has clusters of yellow, blue and pink flowers, daffodils, and pink roses on black.

DELPHINIUM CHINTZ is recognizable by its bright purple and pink delphiniums, abloom on a creamy background.

DORSET was named for an English county, and has widely spaced yellow petunias on a busy, leafy background of tiny magenta flowers. Magenta is the predominant color.

ELEANOR was a popular rose design, with pink, blue, yellow and white accenting flowers on a light background.

ENGLISH ROSE is more subdued, with pink roses and pale blue flowers on a creamy yellow background. The pieces are gilt-edged.

ESTELLE shows a bright and cheerful collection of pink, yellow and lavender flowers on a light colored background, accented by green leaves.

ESTHER is a colorful and dramatic collection of deep pink roses, geraniums, tiny blue flowers and buttercups on a black background.

EVESHAM has the brightly colored fruit of the Evesham orchards in Central England—apples, cherries, figs, grapes, oranges, pears, plums and pomegranates. The design is on a pale background.

EXOTIC BIRD, unlike Birds and Tulips, features vividly colored birds perched in flowering trees. Reds, yellows and blues contrast the creamy background. There is an "Atlas" backstamp on these pieces.

FERNESE consists of white ferns and butterflies against a blue background.

FIREGLOW comes on either a black or white background. This pattern has green leaves with orange, white and blue flowers on black; or pink roses, yellow daffodils, and small blue and yellow flowers on white.

FLORAL FEAST is more widely spaced, showing a mixed bouquet of blue, orange, pink and yellow flowers on a creamy background.

FLORAL GARDEN contains a variety of flowers on a green background.

FLORENCE'S bright, splashy colors are popular with collectors. A black background peeks through large pink, white and creamy flowers, accented by smaller flowers of pink and blue.

HAZEL has a black background with yellow daffodils and roses. The Welbeck pattern is similar, but on a cream background.

JACOBEAN is an early chintz design, more widely spaced according to Victorian fashion. It has pastel vine leaves and red grapes on a black background, and was modeled after a 17th century tapestry.

JACOBINA consists of a mauve, blue or olive green background, with large pink and yellow roses and fuchsia-like flowers.

JOYCE LYNN has a blue background with yellow and pink flowers.

JULIA is another brightly colored mixed bouquet in reds, pinks and yellows on a blue background.

JUNE FESTIVAL is a peony pattern. It has pale pink and yellow posies on a magenta background.

JUNE ROSES is very much like English Rose, featuring shades of pink and yellow on a pale yellow background.

KEW was named after Kew Gardens, a famous tourist site near London, with more than 45,000 species and varieties of plants. The pattern shows red, blue and yellow on an ivory background.

KINVER was named after a small town near Stourbridge Heath and Woodland, England. Deep pink chrysanthemums and roses rest on a creamy background.

MAJESTIC is a design of blues and rosy pink on a black background.

MARGUERITE has various flowers in yellow and deep rose, with purple delphiniums on a white background.

MARION may have been named after Leonard Grimwade's first wife, who died at a young age. It has a cream-colored pebbly background with yellow roses and pink petunias.

MAYFAIR was named after a highly fashionable area of London. Deep pink and yellow chrysanthemums contrast with blue flowers on a creamy background.

MAY FESTIVAL is a peony pattern with white flowers on a black background, similar to June Festival.

MINTON consists of tiny blue flowers on a white background, and a cobalt border with Phoenix birds.

MORNING GLORY has white morning glories on a magenta or black background. It is also found with blue, yellow and pink morning glories on black. Similar in coloring to June Festival.

NANTWICH was named after an old salt mining town in Cheshire, England. It is a busy pattern with orange and pink on black.

OLD COTTAGE CHINTZ has green leaves, red roses, and round, petaled flowers on a light background outlined with grey pebbles.

ORIENTAL FANTASY shows a glossy black background with a pagoda on stylized landscaping.

PAISLEY comes in two different colorings: blues and browns; or green, tan and dark blue. It was named after a town in Scotland.

PEBBLES serves more as a background for other designs than a pattern. It has no flowers, only different sized pebbles on a colored backing.

PEKIN is another Oriental pattern on black, with a stylized Oriental scene. It was also made on ivory, red or green backgrounds.

PELHAM consists of urns of blue, pink and green flowers on a white, cross-hatched background. It is a smaller version of Sampler.

PEONY consists of white peonies on a black background, similar to May Festival.

QUEEN ANNE was named for the reigning queen of England from 1702 to 1714. It has sprigs of red and yellow on a criss-crossed background.

QUILT is a patchwork of many patterns in lavender, pink, blue and black, with a hint of yellow and ivory.

RICHMOND was named after a number of English towns. It has orange-centered yellow and white flowers on a green background.

ROSALIND has red, blue and yellow flowers with green leaves around the edge of each piece. There is a pebbles design in the center.

ROSE DUBARRY has small, not so tightly packed blue and pink flowers on a light colored background.

ROSE SPRIG consists of widely spaced red rose sprigs on a yellow background.

ROYALTY has blue and deep red flowers, with a touch of green, orange and blue. The background can be buttery yellow or black.

RUTLAND was named for an English county. It has white or orange yellow-centered daisies and scattered blue and rose-colored flowers.

SAMPLER resembles an old-fashioned embroidery sampler. Similar to Pelham, this pattern has blue urns of flowers on a white background with criss-crossed lines.

SHREWSBERRY has roses and daisies on a white background.

SOMERSET was named after an English county. The pattern features green, yellow and orange on ivory with tiny clusters of pink and blue posies.

SPRING has pink, red, yellow and blue on an ivory background, with gilding around the edges of each piece.

SPRING GLORY is a subdued pattern in gold, pale blue and pink with pale green leaves on a black background.

SPRINGTIME consists of purple and yellow tulips with green leaf sprays and blue forget-me-nots on white.

STRATFORD was named after the English village

which Shakespeare made famous. It has red tulips and tiny clusters of lavender flowers on white.

SUMMERTIME was called a floral fantasy when it was first introduced. It has a white background with scattered roses in shades of pink and yellow.

SUNSHINE has pinks, blues and sunshine yellow on a cream background.

SWEET NANCY has smaller red and yellow flowers with green leaves, on a cream background.

SWEET PEA consists of blues, yellows and pinks on a creamy yellow background.

TARTANS, like its name, has a Scottish look. It resembles a brightly colored patchwork quilt with pieces in a variety of plaids.

VICTORIAN resembles a needlework pattern. It has a cross-hatched black background, with yellow, red and green bouquets.

VICTORIAN ROSE has an ivory background with orange, lavender and deep pink flowers. This pattern is not closely spaced.

VIOLETS, true to its name, features violets, yellow daffodils and green leaves on a pale background.

WELBECK was named after Welbeck Abbey in Nottinghamshire, England, famous for its 19th century underground passages. This design has yellow and pink roses on a cream background. It is like the Hazel pattern, on a cream background.

WHITE ROSES is a neutral pattern, with a pale yellow background, and roses in white and grey.

WILD FLOWERS is a floral design with pink, blue and yellow flowers, and big white daisies.

WINIFRED consists of brown and tan shades with large yellow and red-pink roses on a pale, leafy background.

LUSTRE CHINTZ

Some say that lustre is not true chintz. However it does meet the criteria of all-over design transfer ware, so I have included it here. Lustre chintz can be found in tea sets and serving pieces, some of them with Rosebud handles and finials. These pieces featured the round Royal Winton backstamp used from 1934–50, and the straight line backstamp used from 1951 onward.

BROCADE

Brocade is a coral colored lustre design on silvery grey. Heavily gilded, Brocade appears to be a variation on the Dorset pattern. These pieces feature the straight line backstamp used from 1951 onward.

QUILTED ROSE

Quilted Rose Chintz has large white roses on a quilted background. It comes in pale blue, cranberry, cream, green and rouge red. It has also been called Quilted Lustre, Quilted Rose, Lustre Rose and Rosepoint. Quilted Rose seems to be an appropriate description. Examples of these and other chintz patterns are illustrated on pages 34–38.

COMMEMORATIVE AND PATRIOTIC WARE

Commemorative items were manufactured to recognize war heroes, Royal coronations and other events that warranted public interest. Royal Winton's commemorative items included plates, bowls, tankards, compotes, cups and saucers, decorated with the image of a current monarch or wartime hero. They produced coronation pieces in 1902, 1911, 1936 and 1953 whenever a new monarch was expected to take the throne.

Patriotic ware was made during the grim years of World War I, intended to bring cheer to the soldiers fighting for their country, and to their families waiting at home. These pieces were stamped "Made by the girls of Staffordshire during the Great War when the 'boys' were in the Trenches fighting for Liberty and Civilization." Today, they are not easy to find.

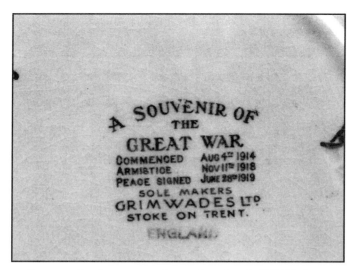

Patirotic backstamp on the underside of a WWI plate.

Another backstamp commonly appearing on Patriotic Ware.

Some pieces had reproductions of Bairnsfather cartoons. Captain Bruce Bairnsfather, an officer in the Royal Warwickshire Regiment during World War I, was a popular British cartoonist who created black and white humorous sketches of war at the front. These sketches, which he sent home to England, were later published in book form, entitled *Fragments from France*. Some were reproduced on commemorative mugs and plates, featuring "Old Bill" with a companion.

Royal Winton's commemorative pieces from World War II carried the likeness of Prime Minister Winston Churchill, President Franklin D. Roosevelt, Lord Beatty (Admiral of the Royal Fleet), and Lord Douglas Haig (General of the Royal Army). It was General Haig who suggested the custom of poppies being sold in Britain on Remembrance Sunday— the Sunday closest to November 11 (what Americans call Veteran's Day)—commemorating the end of World War I. The idea probably came from a popular and poignant poem about the site of a very bloody WWI battle at Flanders, Belgium:

"In Flanders fields the poppies blow
Between the crosses, row on row . . ."
"Flanders Fields"
—John McCrae, 1915

These pieces featured the Grimwades world stamp used from 1930 onward. Examples of commemorative and patriotic ware can be seen above, and on pages 40–41.

COTTAGE AND RELIEF WARE

Cottage ware has also been called English Majolica. *Webster's New Collegiate Dictionary* defines majolica as "earthenware covered with an opaque tin glaze and decorated on the glaze before firing; an Italian ware of this kind; a 19th century earthenware modeled in naturalistic shapes and glazed in lively colors."

The technique for making majolica first came to Spain from Italy in the 14th century, shipped via the small island of Majorca. From Spain, it came to England where British potters admired and emulated the technique. In 1851, at Stoke-on-Trent, Minton Pottery produced the first English Majolica, which proved to be very popular. Royal Winton was one of the other Potteries that followed suit in the 20th century, producing brightly colored pottery with a lumpy, bumpy look. In their *Price Guide to Majolica*, L-W Book Sales and Publishing states that English Potteries, including Grimwades, used transparent lead bases rather than opaque tin bases in their formula.

Also called cottage ware (because the items were shaped like small cottages), Royal Winton made its majolica in the 1930s, some pieces with the round Rubian backstamp used from 1934 to 1950 (indicating they were made at Grimwades' Rubian Art Pottery). They were not always marked, but Royal Winton's pieces had a distinctive coloring which made them stand out from other Potteries'. Imaginatively created in strong colors like brown, green, blue, orange and red, Royal Winton cottage ware offered a whimsical way to brighten the breakfast table on a cold or dreary morning. Royal Winton cottage ware was made in the 1930s.

Cottage pieces included Anne Hathaway's Cottage, Olde Mill with a pink or red roof, Olde England, and Olde Inne with a lilac or red roof. Other pieces in the category included Chanticleer (French for rooster); Lakeland on a yellow or lilac background; a Beehive in primrose, honey or lilac; and a red or green Pixie. Roosters and hens were depicted on a patch of grass and colored in striking hues. Some collectors only look for pieces with a certain coloring.

Company advertising from the 1930s shows that Royal Winton made relief ware to include condiment sets, cruet sets, covered butter and cheese keepers, biscuit barrels, egg cups, marmalades, jugs, sugars, sugar sifters, dessert plates, teapots, toast racks, tea sets (consisting of a teapot, hot water jug, creamer and sugar) and trivets (early metal hot pads or dish holders).

They also made vegetable and serving dishes, as well as celery dishes that resembled wrinkled lettuce leaves. Molded relief ware (or bas relief) came in Royal Winton's more familiar pastels, with molded handles in the shape of flowers. Patterns included Regina, Primula and Gera. These pieces featured a different backstamp, indicating "Made In England" and the name of the piece. Examples of cottage and relief ware are illustrated on pages 42–44 and 62–67.

GOLDEN AND SILVER AGE (LUSTRE)

These gold and silver pieces were intended to imitate gold and silver-plated metal. They were made by application of a thin metallic film of gold oxide (for gold color) or platinum (for silver color). Copper lustre came from copper oxide.

Tea sets, bowls, plates, trays, wall pockets and trinket boxes are all highly collectible. As with other lustre ware, these were probably made for special occasions, rather than for everyday use. Examples of golden and silver age can be seen on pages 56–57.

HANDPAINTED WARE

Most Potteries produced handpainted china in their early years, but Royal Winton introduced a different style of handpainted pieces after World War II. These decorated and gilded items included vases, bowls and jardinieres, not so much intended for everyday use as for display. Many of Royal Winton's lustre pieces were also handpainted in this fashion. Generally, painted transfer ware was also considered handpainted if it was unusual or large in size. These pieces featured the round Royal Winton backstamps used from 1934 to 1950. Illustrated on pages 45–47.

HOUSEHOLD AND PATENT ITEMS

At the turn of the Century, electric lights, bathrooms, and running water in every home were commodities of a more luxurious future. Before these conveniences became commonplace, every home

Backstamp commonly found on Golden Age items made after 1945. This piece has an "A" below the trademark.

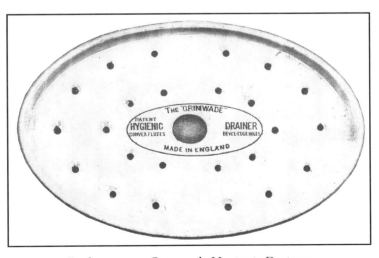

Backstamp on Grimwade Hygienic Drainer.

Of their many patented items, Grimwade/Royal Winton was well known for their ceramic bed pans. This one shows a 1950s backstamp.

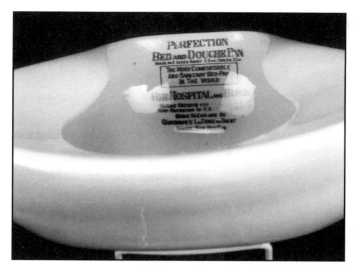

"The Most Comfortable and Sanitary Bed-Pan in the World." The Perfection Bed and Douche Pan.

The Mecca Hot Water Bottle, another item admired by Queen Mary during her 1913 visit.

Grimwades Quick-Cooker Bowl, admired by Queen Mary during her 1913 Royal visit to the Potteries with King George V.

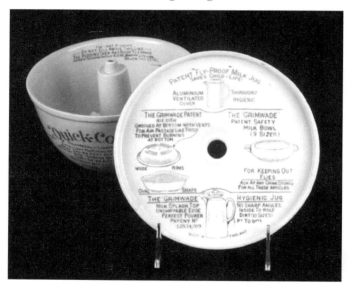

required hygienic items such as washstand bowls and pitchers, toothbrush holders, soap and sponge dishes, and chamber pots that sat under the bed or in a stand beside the bed. As homes became modernized, many of these hygienic items were no longer manufactured, except for decorative or hospital purposes.

Royal Winton had long been a leader in the production of ceramic hygienic items, and was said to be the biggest producer of bed pots in the world. Richard Llewelyn Grimwade, one of Sidney's great-grandsons, laughed as he recalled a family joke about the famous Grimwade bed pots. "My father always said bed pots were the source of Grimwades' fortune. He said the company failed when Sir Arthur Crapper invented the inside toilet."

On the contrary, not only did Grimwades manufacture countless other household items, the company went on to become the foremost (and most widely copied) producer of chintz ware in the 1930s and '40s.

There were Royal Winton ceramic hot water bottles used as foot warmers for cold winter beds, covered with a decorative cloth or towel to prevent any burns from the hot ceramic. Dresser trays, trinket boxes, pin trays and hair receivers were other

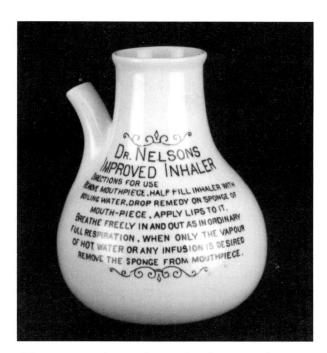

Many patented items featured enthusiastic descriptions and step-by-step instructions on each piece, such as on this "Dr. Nelson's Improved Inhaler."

items considered a necessary part of comfortable living; as were chamber sticks and candlesticks with finger holes, to light the way to the bedroom in the dark of night.

Traditionally, the kitchen was the heart of the home, and it took a remarkable variety of special dishes and containers to produce the family meals and maintain a household. These included jelly and blancmange molds, fluted pudding bowls, lemon squeezers, pie funnels, square fitted pie bakers of different sizes, and more, all of which Royal Winton supplied.

Items were patented to make cooking easier and more sanitary. Royal Winton produced a Quick-Cooker bowl in five sizes, with a grooved lid that eliminated the need for unsanitary pudding cloths. Other patented items included a tea machine with a valve-operated infuser; a sanitary milk bowl in which to store milk; a pie dish with ring grooves; a hygienic drainer; and their Paragon coffee pot with a removable strainer (named "paragon" to indicate how splendid it was). Today, these collectibles give us a peek at the life, times and flavor of English households of the past. Backstamps usually carried the name of the piece. Examples of household and patent items can be seen on pages 48–49.

LEAF WARE (MAPLE LEAF)

Leaf ware appeared in the late 1950s and throughout the '60s. It included dishes, creamer and sugar sets, and trays shaped like maple leaves. Leaf ware pieces had a different backstamp and a heavier, sturdier look than most Royal Winton wares. Straight line Royal Winton stamp with an "A" underneath. They were made in pale shades of brown, cream and green, unlike the usually vibrant Royal Winton pastels.

It seems likely that this pattern was intended for export to Canada because of the maple leaf motif, and because it can be found there in abundance (it tended to be plain and less expensive than earlier pieces). The pattern is scarce in the United States and England. Some leaf ware made in the 1950s was gilded. Illustrated on pages 50–51.

LUSTRE WARE

Made primarily in the 1930s, and again in the '40s, lustre ware pieces were beautifully shaded in a rainbow of color including soft yellow, blue, green, deep magenta and cream. Colors varied from piece to piece, alternating strong, subtle shades with metallic silver and gold, and even abstract designs hand-traced in gold.

Like Byzanta, lustre described a decorative effect rather than a pattern, and was evident in wares from other Royal Winton lines. The Shakespeare Series (from the Byzanta line) was made in mottled rust-colored lustre, pale mottled green and blue. The backstamp shows a picture of the Bard, with an illustration on each piece depicting Shakespearean characters such as Orlando and Rosalind.

Lustre pieces were limited for the most part to special occasions or decorative use, and included tea sets, cups and saucers, creams and sugars, sherbets, jam jars, wall pockets, bowls and vases. Examples of Lustre ware are shown on pages 52–55.

MOTTLED WARE

Mottled ware has also been called marbled, spackled and speckled ware. If the majority rules, then mottled ware seems to be the proper name. It has also been called pastel ware; however, since pastel refers to pieces with pale coloring, the rouge red mottled pieces do not really qualify. Royal Winton made this pattern in pink, cranberry, green, yellow and rouge red. Shapes and items made include teapots, tea sets, sherbets, jam jars, wall pockets, bowls, vases, bedside and breakfast sets, and almost any item that was made in chintz ware. These pieces featured the Royal Winton backstamps used from 1951 onward. Examples of mottled ware are shown on page 58.

MUGS AND JUGS

It is possible that the word "mug"—slang for "face"—originated from these character pieces. Royal Winton's mugs portrayed wartime heroes and other characters of public interest. Although Royal Winton made thousands of character mugs, theirs are not as easy to find as those from other Potteries. They were only manufactured for a brief period of time, from the late 1930s to the mid-1940s, and came in four sizes: large (7" or larger), medium (6–6$\frac{1}{2}$"), small (3$\frac{1}{2}$") and tiny (3" or smaller).

Royal Winton's mugs offered carefully painted and detailed portraits, with particular attention paid to the handles. Their Uncle Sam mug had a dollar symbol for a handle, while military figures had swords. Military details, in general, were faithfully presented.

Notable characters portrayed on these mugs included Royal and political personages, and military heroes, both real and imagined. For example: King George VI appeared on one mug in military uniform; John Bull—Britain's equivalent of Uncle Sam—on another. There were mugs depicting

Prime Minister Winston Churchill; Field Marshal Smuts; Franklin D. Roosevelt; General Douglas MacArthur; General Sir Arthur Wavell; a Native American Chief in full feathered headdress; Mr. Winkle; Mr. Pickwick; a character called Old Jarvie; and a Canadian mountie.

One of Richard Grimwade's prized family possessions is a John Bull mug. Most of the mugs were created realistically, like a sculptured portrait, but some were undecorated, such as a mug depicting King Henry VIII. These may have been seconds, damaged in some way, or made after World War II when production of decorated items was curtailed.

Character mugs should not be confused with Toby jugs, although the terms are often used interchangeably. Typically, character mugs showed the head and shoulders of the character portrayed, and were used for drinking. The Toby jugs featured a

The Olde Jarvie mug, 3$\frac{3}{4}$" high. The character mug of King George VI was left undecorated. Also 3$\frac{3}{4}$" high.

This photograph confirms that Royal Winton made four different sizes of character mugs.

standing or seated figure wearing a tri-cornered hat, which formed a spout for pouring. The figure held a jug on one knee and a glass in his other hand.

There are several suggestions as to the origin of the name Toby, which dates back to the 18th century. Perhaps the jug was named after a character called Uncle Toby, in Lawrence Stern's book *Tristian Sandy*. Or, after a character named Toby Fillpot from a popular British song. The latter is more logical, since the jugs were also called fillpots for a time.

Beer and cider mugs were created from the 1930s, some in relief, others with a musical feature. The musical mugs were designed to play a tune when picked up, typical tunes including "God Save Our Gracious King," and "Here's Health to His Majesty." One depicts a tipsy man leaning on a lamp post, and plays "How Dry I Am." Relief mugs had detailed landscapes and handles, portraying historic, Royal or village scenes.

Royal Winton also made gurgling jugs, which were popular and widely copied items. They were designed for pub use, with hollow handles that made a gurgling sound whenever water was poured from them. The jugs added to the pub's entertainment value. These pieces featured both the round and straight line Royal Winton backstamps used from 1934 onward, with the words "Gurgling Jug." Examples of mugs and jugs can be seen on page 59.

Pip the Panda backstamp, one of the character series featured on Royal Winton's nursery ware.

NURSERY WARE

From its early years (1886–1913), Royal Winton produced a variety of nursery ware designed to entertain and teach, making mealtime special for children. Illustrated Mother Goose nursery rhymes became popular in the 1800s, as well as pictures of black cats, imps and Brownies. Soon this motif was applied to ceramic ware.

In 1883, author/artist Palmer Cox wrote and illustrated a poem, "The Brownies Ride," followed by a series of books, *The Brownies, Their Books*. Brownies were used as popularly then as Disney characters are today. In Scottish folklore, they were benevolent elves and fairies who secretly performed domestic chores while the members of a household slept. In appreciation, a bowl of milk was set out for the Brownies each evening.

These delightful little elves captured the imagination of the public. By the late 1890s, they were widely used in advertising in England, similar to our 20th century cartoon characters. The popular Brownie Camera took its name from them, as did the Girl Scout Brownies, whose goal, like Brownies, was that of being helpful. They appeared on children's games and nursery dishes, many of which were made by Royal Winton.

Other Royal Winton nursery ware featured their Charles Dickens series, *Aesop's Fables*, *Robinson Crusoe*, "Old Country" nursery rhymes, piggies, bubbles and balloons. In the 1950s, a bunnies series and "Pip the Panda" were introduced. The backstamps on these items featured the name of the piece or series. Examples of nursery ware are illustrated on page 60.

PASTEL WARE

By definition, the word "pastel" refers to pale, insipid colors. However Royal Winton's pastel line was far from insipid. It came in soft but vibrant cream, green, pink and yellow. Some pieces were undecorated, others enameled or handpainted. This same pastel coloring was also used in the Rosebud line and in mottled ware, along with a deeper shade of rouge. Made in the 1930s, these pieces featured either the world or the curved line Grimwades backstamps. Examples of pastel ware can be seen on pages 61–63.

ROSEBUD WARE

Royal Winton's Rosebud items from the 1940s included tea sets, wall pockets, candlesticks, toast racks and bedside trays. Most pieces were more decorative than practical, with molded handles and knobs in relief, shaped like rosebuds or other small flowers. Briar roses, tiger lilies, petunias, fuchsias, hibiscus and pansies were some of the other flowers used in this charming line of ware, their names frequently printed on the piece. Occasionally, clusters of cherries or peaches were also featured.

Rosebud was made in pastel colors, with handpainted accents and a plain underglaze in pink, green, cream or Buttercup yellow. For Royal Winton collectors, Rosebud pieces make delightful companions for chintz and pastel ware, and are becoming more and more popular as such. These pieces featured the round Royal Winton backstamps used from 1934 to 1950. Illustrated on pages 64–67.

SOUVENIR WARE

Since World War II, tourists from other nations have been fascinated with the English countryside and history, and English Potteries have manufactured portable souvenir items popular with visitors. When it became more common for British travelers to visit Canada and the United States (and for Americans to visit England and Canada), Royal Winton manufactured large quantities of souvenir ware that appealed to visitors whose destinations included those countries as well as British colonies, such as Bermuda. Many of the souvenir items carry the Jon Roth backstamp, indicating they had been handled by this English distributor of Royal Winton in the 1950s.

Plates and dishes were created depicting memorable vacation spots abroad, including Bermuda, Canada, England, Scotland and the United States. There were also vases, pin trays, creamers, sugars, cups, saucers, trinket boxes and other items small enough to transport home as gifts. There were also musical chromed cake stands with pictorial scenes of market or village life. All souvenir ware was made with transfers, while some pieces were handpainted as well. Examples of souvenir ware can be found on pages 68–74.

TRANSFER WARE (NON-CHINTZ)

Non-chintz transfer ware featured floral and fruit designs, garden and village scenes, stagecoaches and hunt scenes. We have seen some simple transfer pieces with backstamps that date pre-1900, indicating early production. But Grimwades began regularly producing transfer ware after acquiring Rubian Art Pottery in 1906, and the technique appeared in different forms throughout the years.

In the 1920s, in recognition of the British discovery and excavation of King Tutankhamen's tomb, designs with an Egyptian motif were introduced. Some transfer pieces were also enameled, easily recognizable since the enamel effect stands out well. Others had hand painting added to the design.

To tell the difference between handpainted and transfer ware, look at the piece through a magnifying glass. There will be brush strokes on a handpainted item, whereas transfer designs show up in tiny dots when magnified. Some transfer pieces that were also handpainted will show both brush strokes and dots. Royal Winton made transfer ware continually until the 1960s, and these pieces featured the entire range of backstamps. Examples of non-chintz transfer ware are shown on pages 73–81.

1

2

3

4

5

6

7

CHINTZ

8

9

10

11

12

13

14

15

16

17

18

19

CHINTZ

19A

20

21

22

23

24

25

26

27

CHINTZ

28

29

30

31

32

33

34

35

36

37

38

CHINTZ

39

40

41

42

43

44

45A

45

46

LUSTRE CHINTZ

47

48

49

50

51

52

53

54

55

56

57

58

COMMEMORATIVE WARE

59

60

61

62

63

64

65

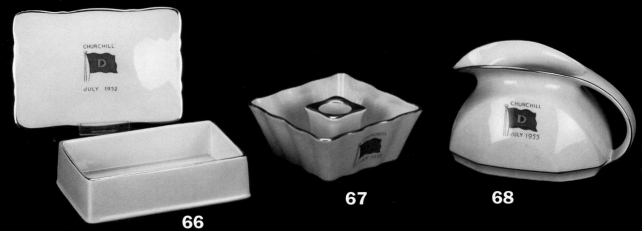

66

67

68

COMMEMORATIVE WARE

69

70

71

72

73

74

75

76

77

78

79

80

81

COTTAGE WARE

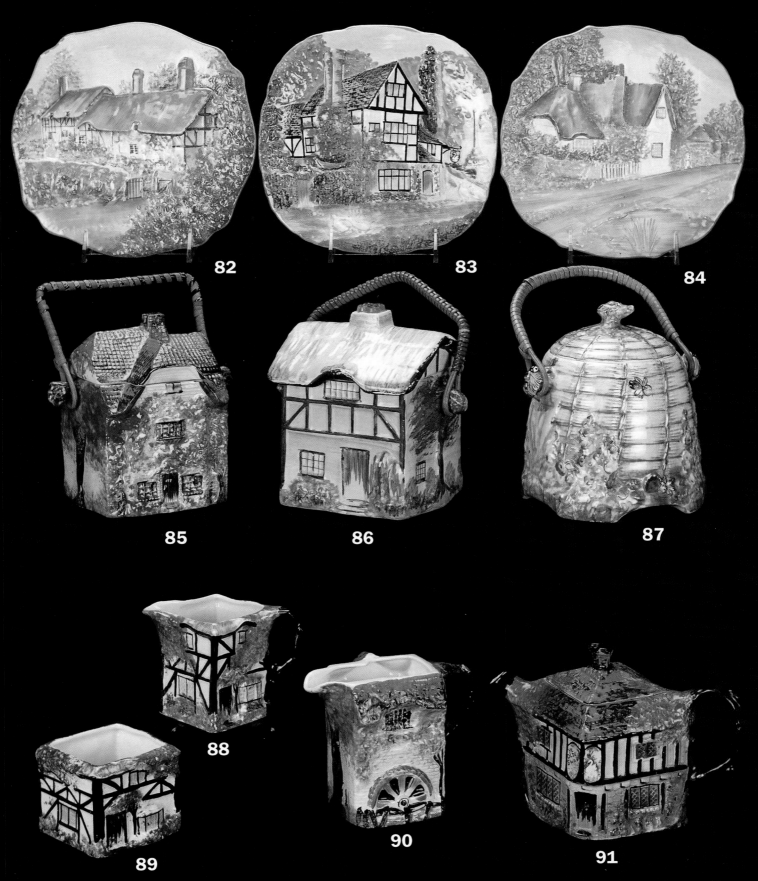

82

83

84

85

86

87

88

89

90

91

COTTAGE WARE

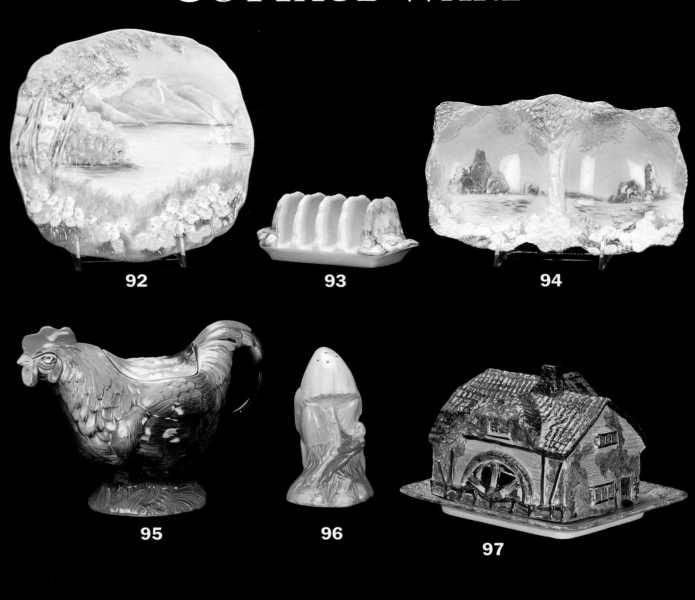

92   93   94

95   96   97

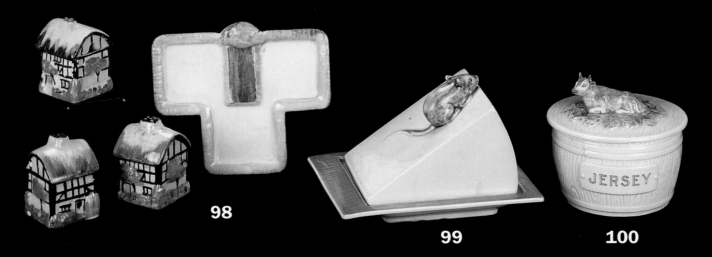

98   99   100

RELIEF WARE

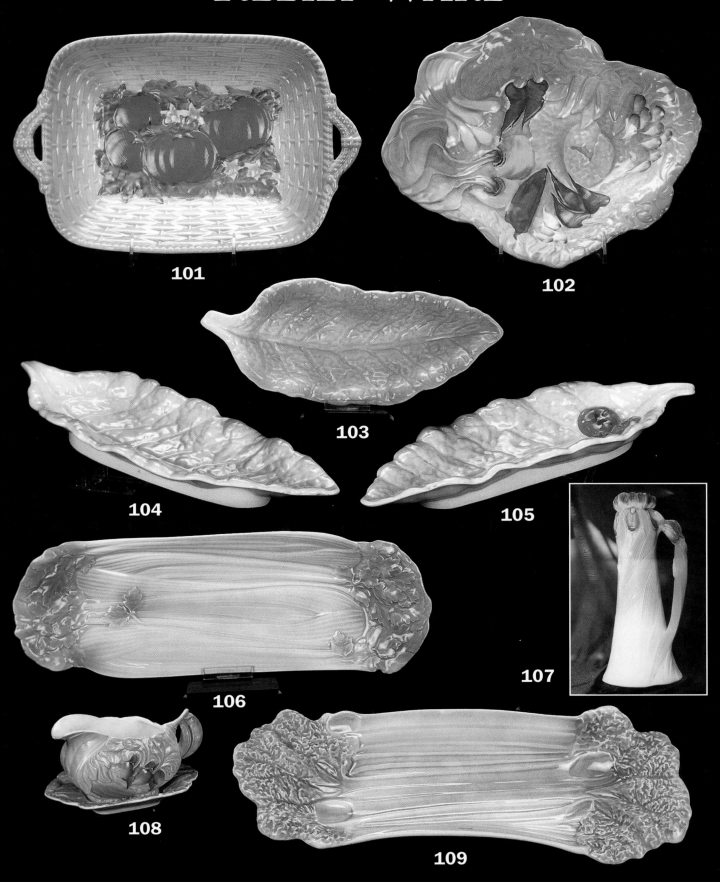

101

102

103

104

105

106

107

108

109

HANDPAINTED

110

111

112

113

114

115

116

117

HANDPAINTED

118

119

120

121

122

123

124

125

HANDPAINTED
Red Roof

126

127

128

129

130

131

132

133

134

135

46

HOUSEHOLD WARE

136

137

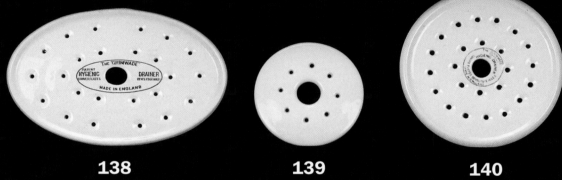

138   **139**   **140**

141   **142**   **143**   **144**

Household Ware

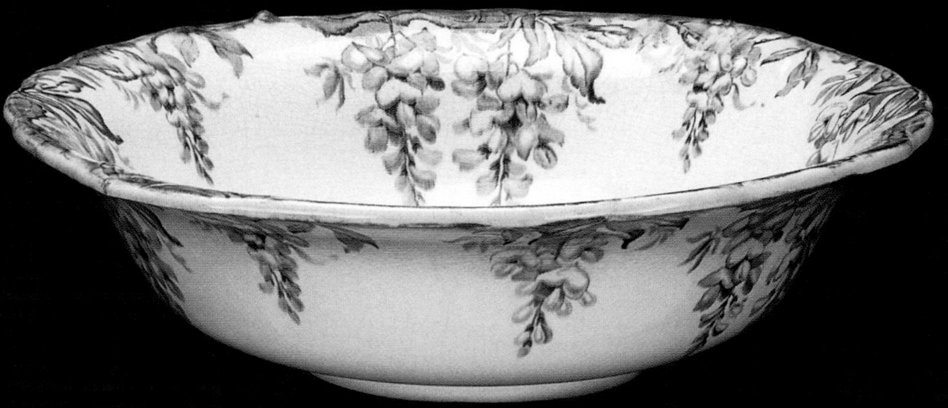

145

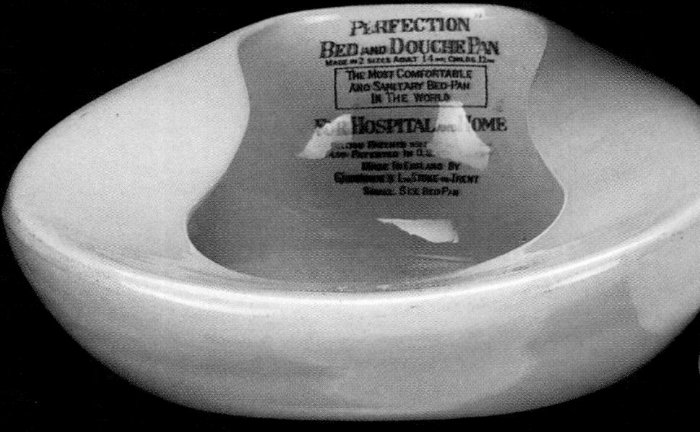
PERFECTION
BED AND DOUCHE PAN
THE MOST COMFORTABLE
AND SANITARY BED-PAN
IN THE WORLD
HOSPITAL
MADE IN ENGLAND BY
SIZE BED PAN

146

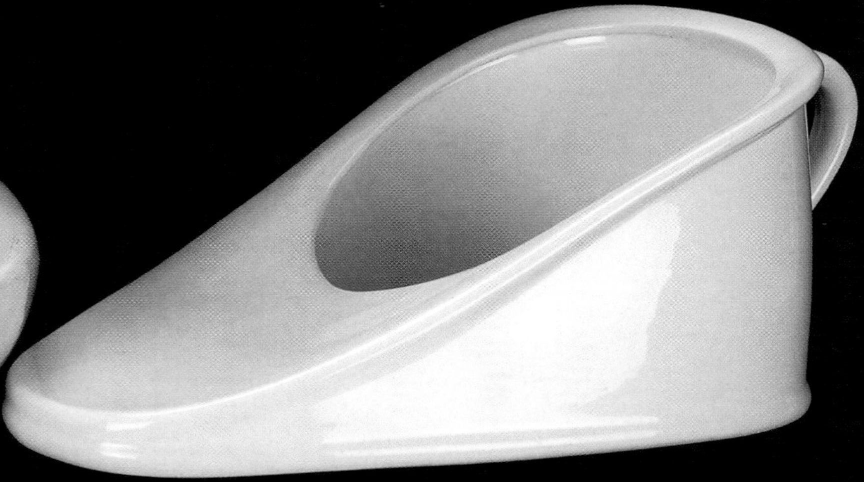

147

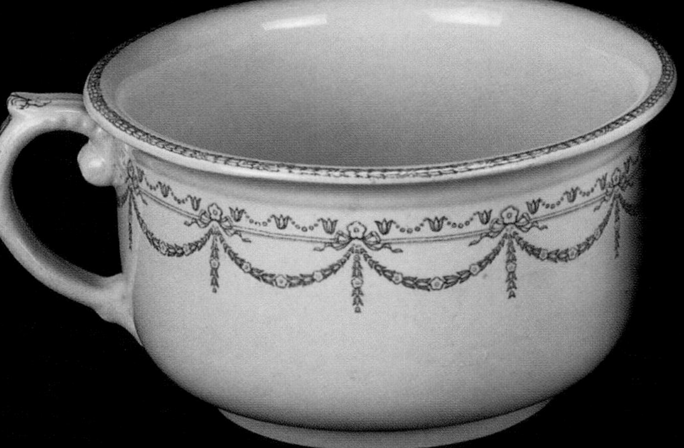

148

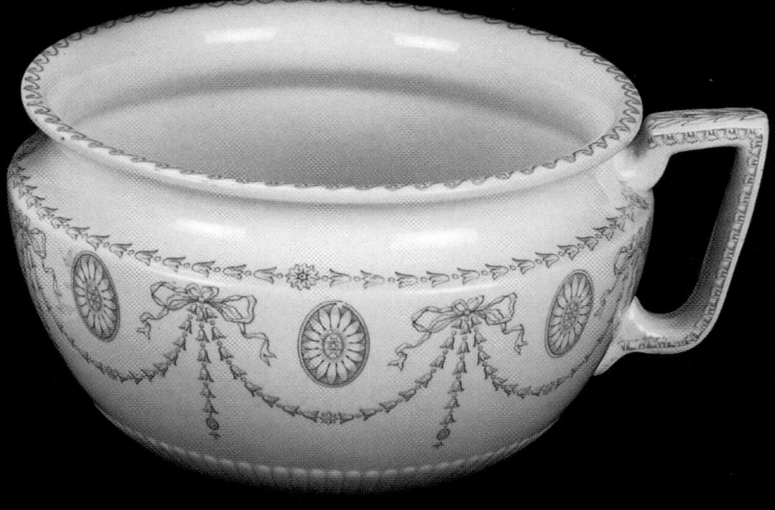

149

LEAF WARE

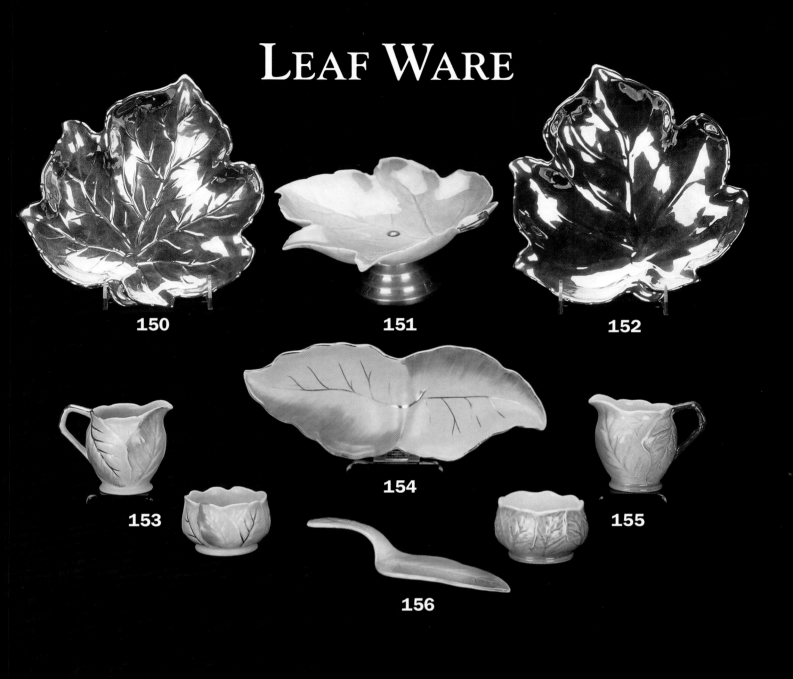

150
151
152

153
154
155

156

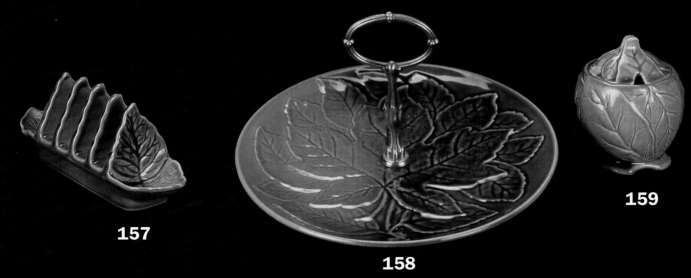

157
158
159

LEAF WARE

160

161

162

163

164

165

166

167

LUSTRE WARE

168

169

170

171

172

173

174

175

176

177

LUSTRE WARE

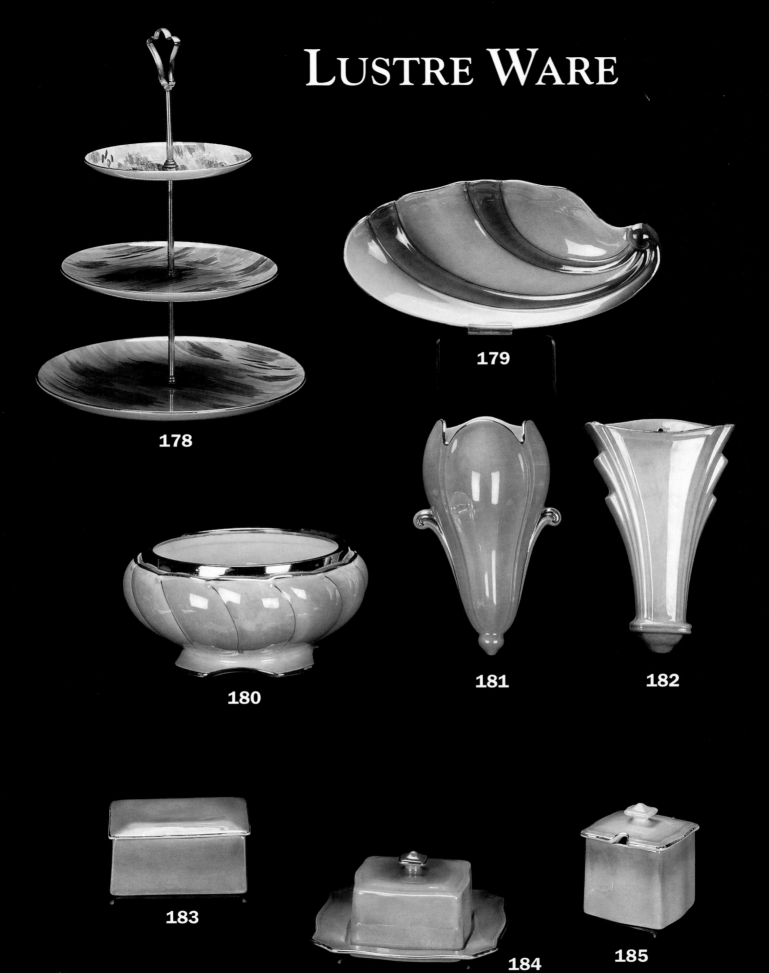

178

179

180

181

182

183

184

185

LUSTRE WARE

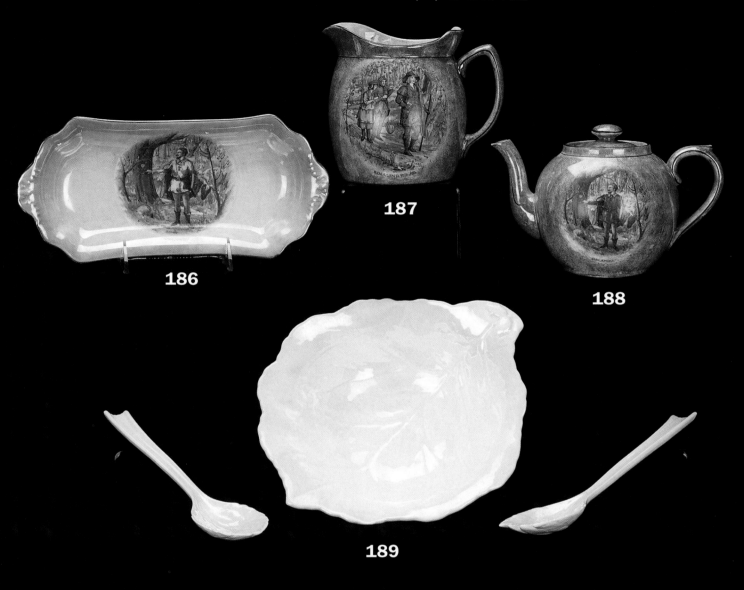

186

187

188

189

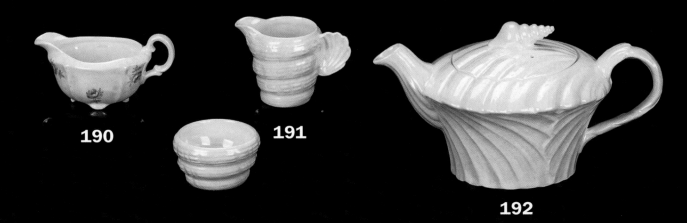

190

191

192

LUSTRE WARE

193

194

195

196

197

198

199

200

201

202

203

204

205

206

GOLDEN AND SILVER AGE

207

208

209

210

211

212

213

214

215

216

217

GOLDEN AGE

218 **219** **220** **221**

222 **223** **224**

225 **226** **227**

228

Mottled Ware

229

230

231

232

233

234

235

236

237

238

239

240

241

242

243

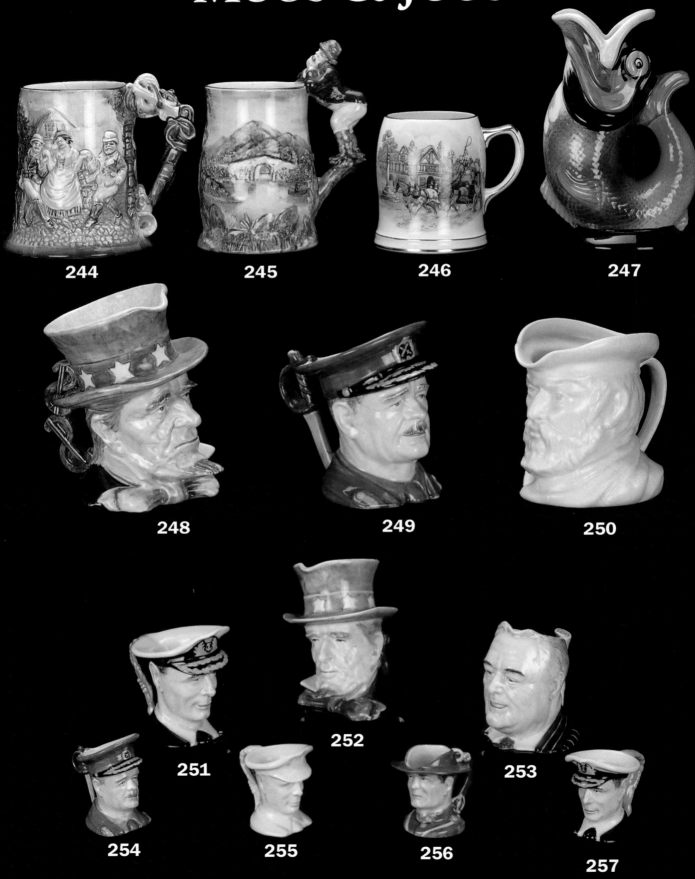

244

245

246

247

248

249

250

251

252

253

254

255

256

257

NURSERY WARE

258

259

260

261

PASTEL

262

263

264

265

266

267

268

269

270

271

272

Pastel/Molded Relief

273

274

275

276

277

278

279

280

281

282

283

284

285

286

287

288

289

290

291

292

293

294

295

296

297

298

299

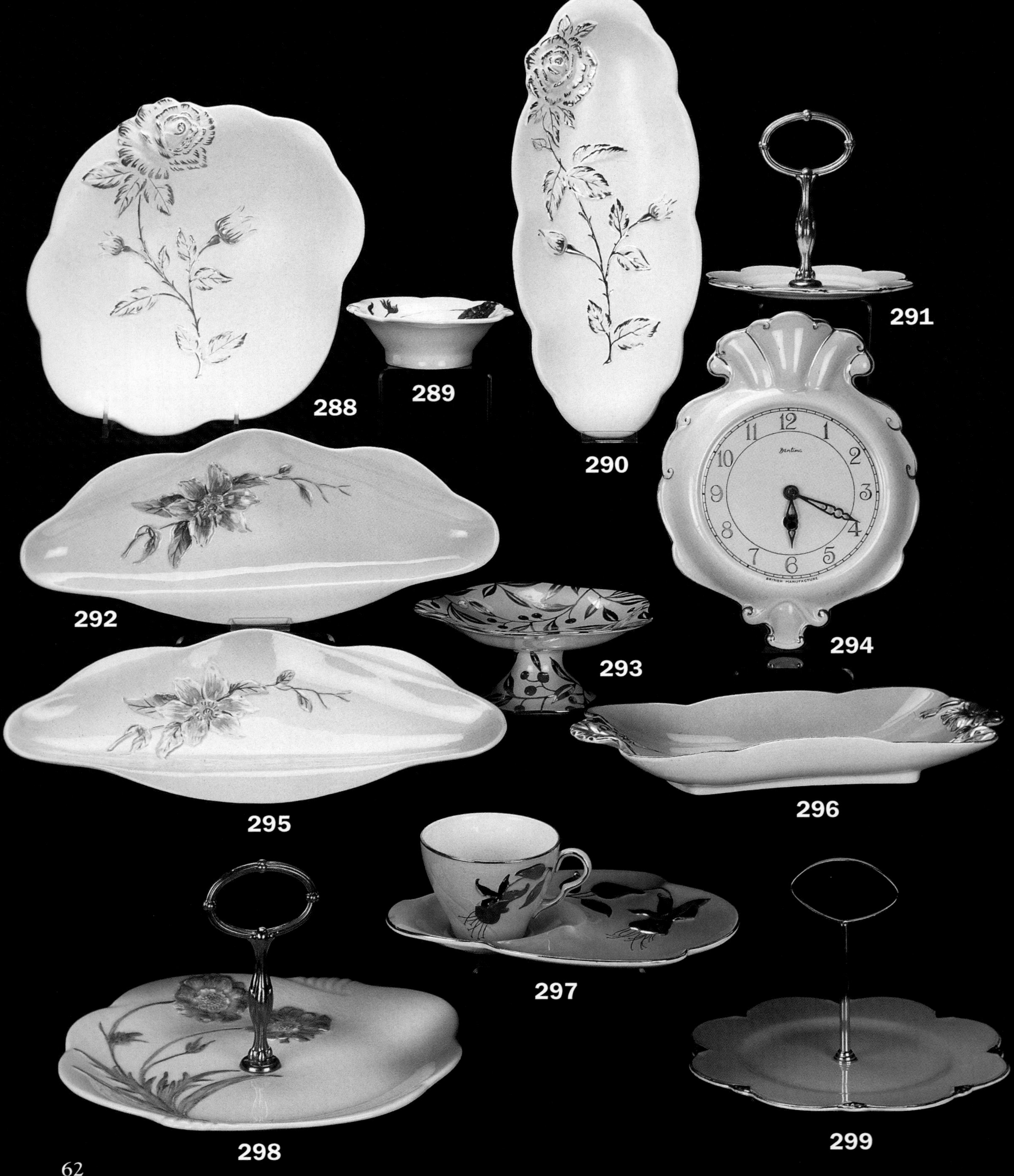

ROSEBUD/MOLDED RELIEF

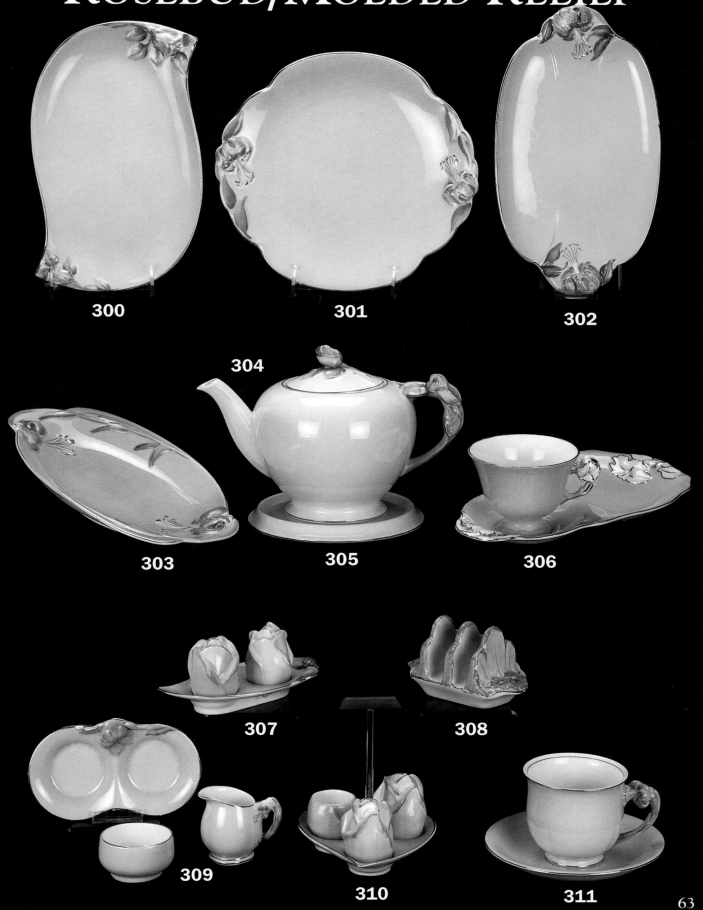

300

301

302

304

303

305

306

307

308

309

310

311

ROSEBUD/MOLDED RELIEF

312

313

314

315

316

317

318

319

320

321

322

ROSEBUD/MOLDED RELIEF

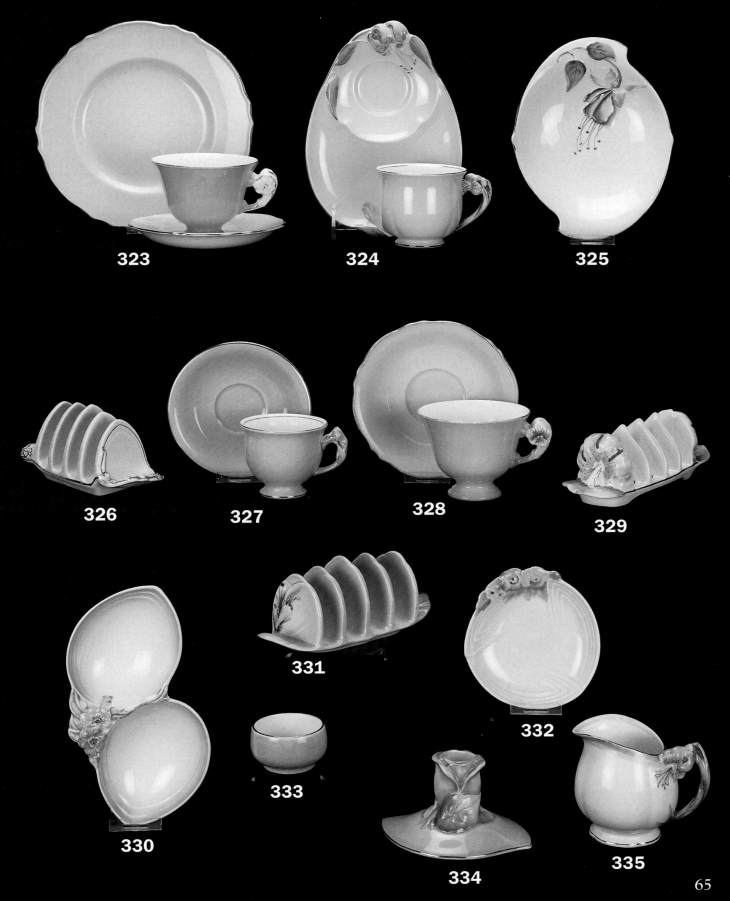

323

324

325

326

327

328

329

330

331

332

333

334

335

336

337

338

339

340

341

342

343

344

345

346

347

SOUVENIR WARE

348

349

350

351

352

353

354

355

356

357

358

359

360

SOUVENIR WARE

361

362

363

364

365

366

367

368

369

370

371

SOUVENIR WARE

372

373

374

375

376

377

378

379

380

381

382

383

384

385

386

387

SOUVENIR WARE

390

388

389

392

393

391

394

395

396

397

398

399

400

401

402

403

404

SOUVENIR WARE

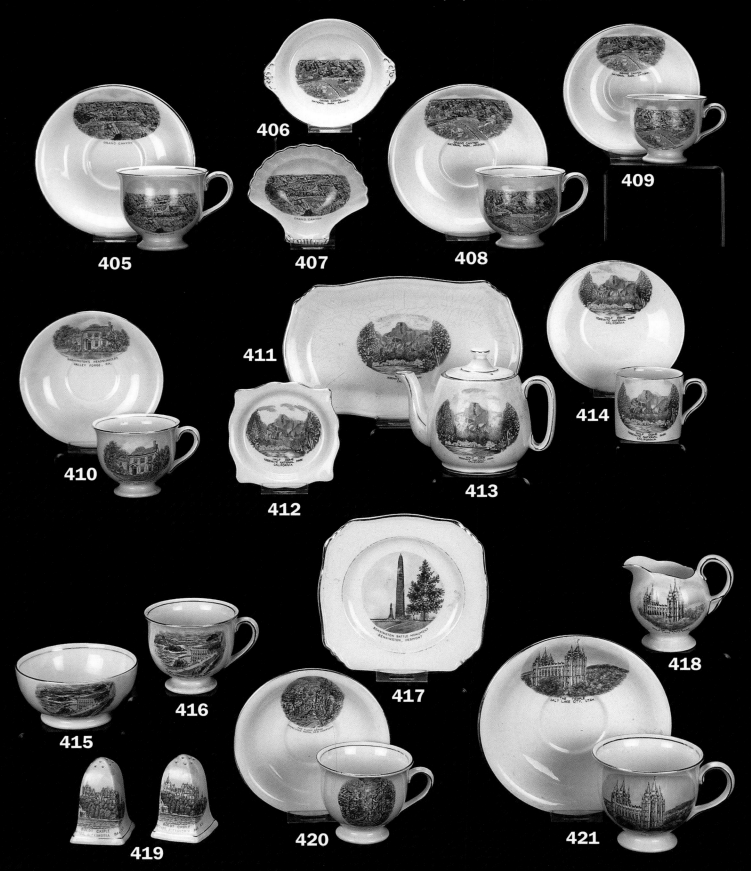

405

406

407

408

409

410

411

412

413

414

415

416

417

418

419

420

421

SOUVENIR TRANSFER

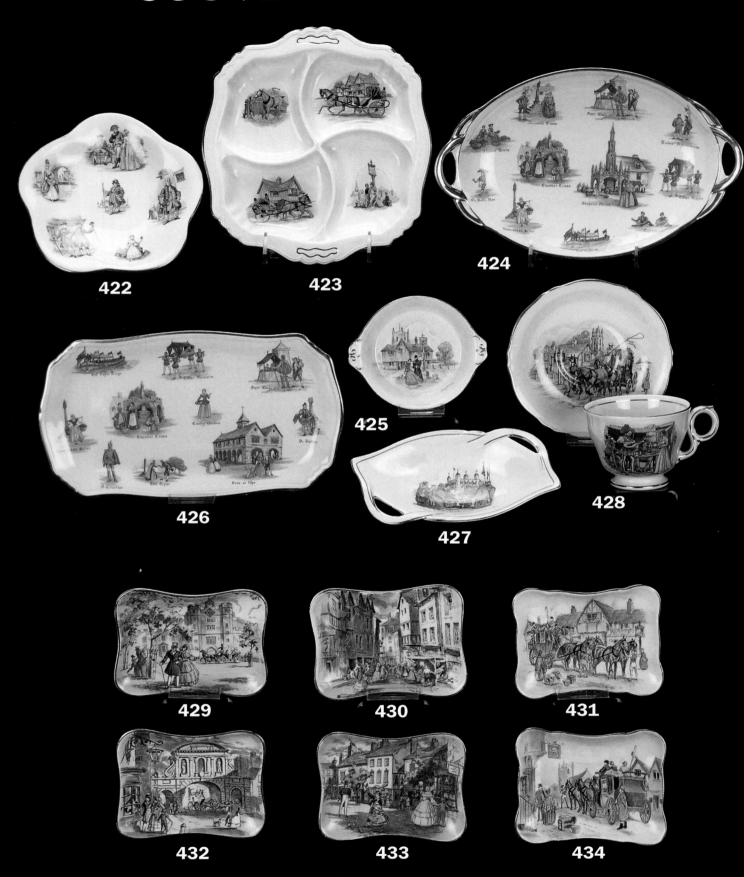

422

423

424

425

426

427

428

429

430

431

432

433

434

SOUVENIR TRANSFER

435

436

437

438

439

440

441

442

443

444

445

TRANSFER WARE

446

447

448

449

450

451

452

453

454

455

Transfer Ware

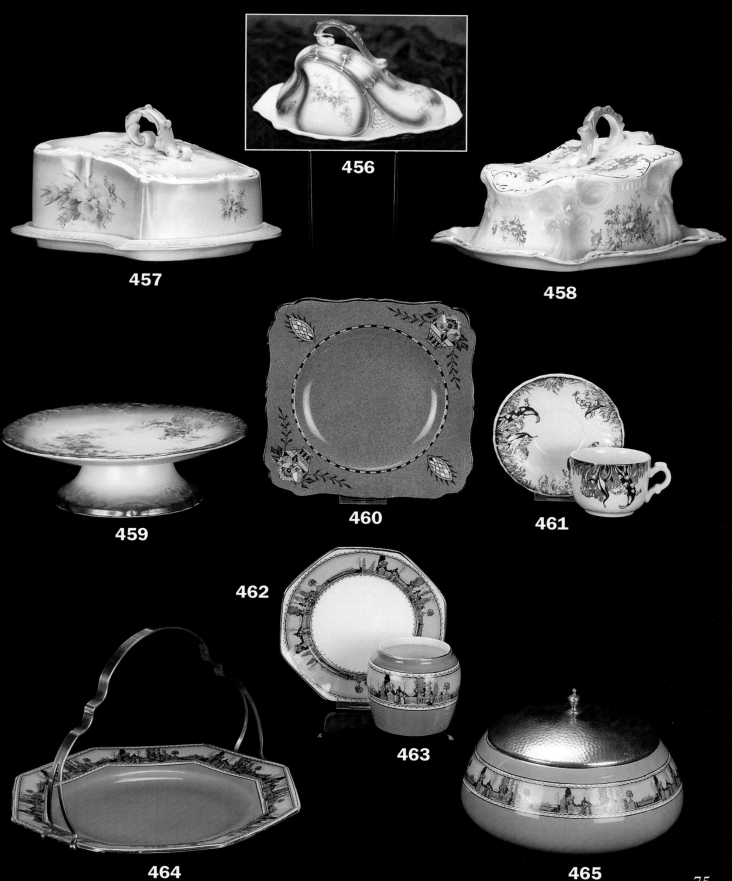

456

457

458

459

460

461

462

463

464

465

Transfer Ware

466

467

468

469

470

471

472

473

474

475

476

477

478

479

480

481

482

483

484

485

486

487

488

489

490

491

492

493

494

495

496

499

497

498

TRANSFER WARE

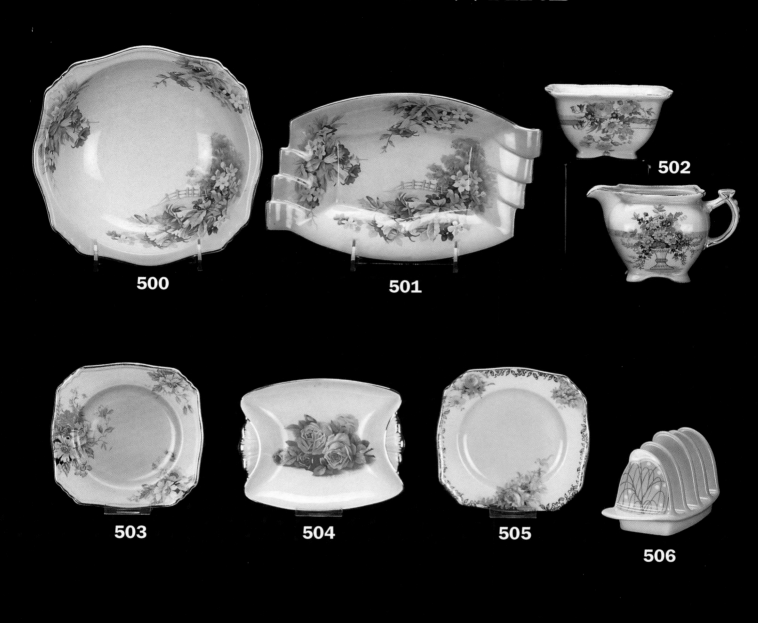

500

501

502

503

504

505

506

507

508

509

510

TRANSFER DINNER SERVICE FOR EIGHT

511

512

513

514

515

516

517

518

519

520

521

Royal Visit to the • •

Staffordshire Potteries.

GRIMWADES

GRIMWADES, Ltd.,

Winton Pottery,

Stoke-on-Trent, Staffs.

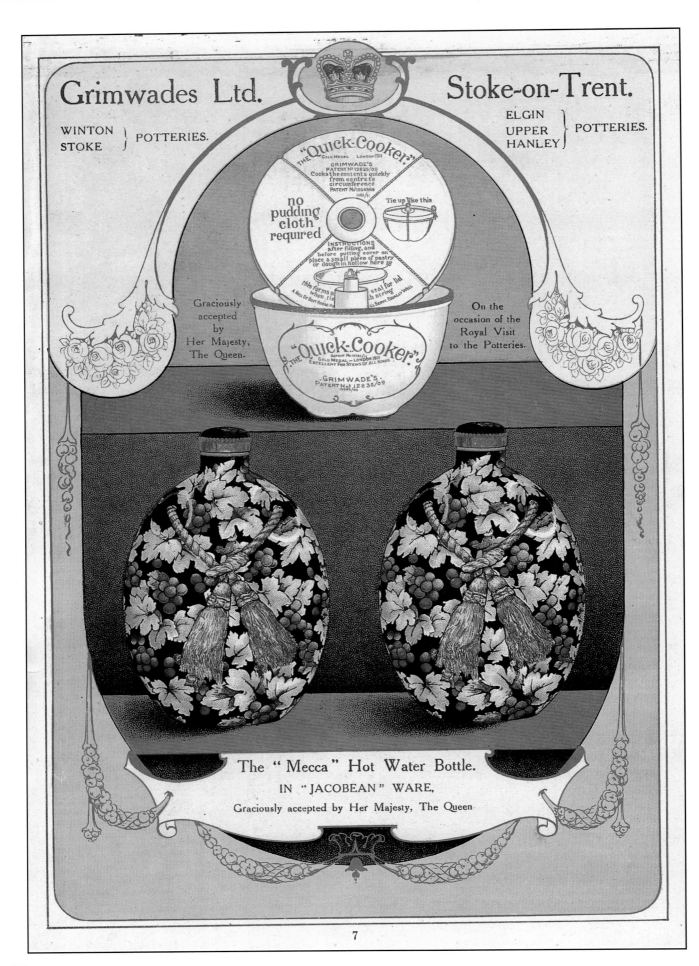

Grimwades Ltd. Stoke-on-Trent.

WINTON } POTTERIES.
STOKE

ELGIN
UPPER } POTTERIES.
HANLEY

"Quick-Cooker."
GOLD MEDAL LONDON 1911
GRIMWADE'S
PATENT No 12835/09
Cooks the contents quickly
from centre to
circumference
PATENT No 13048/09
1161/11

no
pudding
cloth
required

Tie up like this

INSTRUCTIONS
after filling, and
before putting cover on
place a small piece of pastry
or dough in hollow here
this forms a seal for lid
when tied with string

"Quick-Cooker."
PATENT No 13161/L
GOLD MEDAL — LONDON 1911
EXCELLENT FOR STEWS OF ALL KINDS
GRIMWADE'S
PATENT No 12835/09
13048/09

Graciously
accepted
by
Her Majesty,
The Queen.

On the
occasion of the
Royal Visit
to the Potteries.

The " Mecca " Hot Water Bottle.
IN "JACOBEAN" WARE,
Graciously accepted by Her Majesty, The Queen

7

"Jacobean" Ware.

No. 3000. "Bute" Flower Pot.
9 in., 8 in., 7 in., 6 in. and 5 in.

No. 3000. "Delphic" Flower Pot.
8 in., 7 in. and 6 in.

No. 2999. "Octagon"

No. 3000. "Octagon" Shape.

No. 3000. "Silver" Shape.

No. 2999. "Wem"

No. 3000. "Wem" Shape.

No. 3000. "Alton" Shape.

25

"Seville" Ware.

No. 2813.
8 in. and 7 in.

No. 2900.
8 in. and 7 in.

No. 2809.

No. 2813.

No. 2811.

No. 2900.

No. 2812.

No. 2815.

"Hampton" Chintz.

No. 562. "Roma" Shape.

No. 544. "Etona" Shape.

No. 561. "Alton" Shape.

No. 544. "Beaumont" Shape.

No. 564. "Weimar" Shape.

No. 579. "Octagon" Shape.

No. 579. "Riviera" Shape.

No. 561. "Saxe" Shape.

27

85

"Copenhagen" Pattern,

No. 570.

"Niobe" Shape.
9 in. and 8 in.

"Delphic" Shape.
8 in., 7 in. and 6 in.

No. 570.   "Wem" Shape.

No. 570.   "Weimar" Shape.

No. 570.   "Bute" Shape.

No. 570.   "Silver" Shape.

No. 570.   "Alton" Shape.

No. 570.   "Saxe" Shape.

28

"Spode Chintz."

No. 542. "Shan" Shape.

No. 542. "Weimar" Shape.

No. 537. "Weimar"

No. 525. "Etona" Shape.

No. 525. "Kabyle" Shape.

No. 525. "Duval"

No. 542. "Saxe" Shape.

No. 542. "Tara" Shape.

No. 542.
"Mecca" Hot Water Bottle.

30

Solid
Art Toilets.
GUARANTEED
IMPERVIOUS.

"Wem" Shape.
Crushed Strawberry.

"Stuart" Shape.
Crushed Strawberry.

"Stuart" Shape. Turquoise.

"Stuart" Shape. Russian Green.

"Wem" Shape. Dresden Green.

"Tientsin" Shape. Yellow.

"Wem" Shape. Wedgwood Blue.

"Wem" Shape. Heliotrope.

31

COLOR PLATES DESCRIPTIONS

The same shape blanks appear in nearly all categories, decorated differently. Quotation marks indicate the name or markings on a piece. Bowls, compotes, plates, sugars and creamers have been measured for width across the top. Dishes and trays have been measured for length from edge to edge. Covered compotes, covered dishes, jugs, mugs and vases have been measured for height from bottom to top.

BYZANTA, P. 33

1. Floating bowl, 4³/₄" across. Blue lustre inside, brilliant orange with floral design on the outside. Black accent.

2. Vase, 7¹/₂" high. Orange lustre with black bands around the top and bottom. There is a classical musical scene silhouetted in black in the center.

3. Bowl, 6" across. Orange lustre on the outside, yellow lustre on the inside.

4. Covered jam pot with underliner. Blue lustre, gilt-edged. The inner edge is yellow, and the inside of the pot is white.

5. Floating bowl, 4³/₄" across. Blue lustre, with a markete scene inside the bowl.

6. Cup marked "Watteau" on the bottom. There are silhouetted dancers on yellow with a blue-grey tree and city in the background.

7. Bowl, 6" across. Blue lustre, white lustre on the underside. There is a branch with fruit and green leaves inside the bowl.

CHINTZ, PP. 34–37

A few bits and pieces are shown here as pattern examples. Don't turn up your nose when you find these at garage or estate sales. Saucers make handy underliners for glass sherbets, and an open sugar can be used as a nut cup. Odd pieces can sometimes be found to complete a breakfast or condiment set.

8. Birds and Tulips covered butter, marked "Grimwades Ivory."

9. Blue Jade teacup and saucer.

10. Carnation cake plate, 11" across. Marked "Ostria" (probably denoting that it was made to be sold in Australia).

11. Chintz saucer.

12. Chintz open sugar or nut cup.

13. Cloisonne covered butter. Royal Winton mark, but no pattern mark.

14. Cloisonne jam pot. Chrome lid with no underliner. No Royal Winton backstamp, but there is a "Cloisonne" mark.

15. Clyde blue 4-piece condiment set on tray, blue.

16. Bedale plate, 9¹/₂" across.

17. Clyde two-tier cake plate with chrome handle.

18. Dorset salt and pepper. Should come on a tray.

19. Cranstone demitasse cup and saucer.

19A. Estelle saucer.

20. Esther teacup and saucer.

21. Exotic Bird teapot, 6-cup.

22. Exotic Bird creamer and sugar, marked "Atlas."

23. Floral Feast butter tray.

24. Florence vase. This was a 1997 re-issue, included here as a pattern example.

25. Hazel condiment tray, with three indentations.

26. Jacobina candy/sweets dish.

27. Joyce Lynn breakfast tray.

28. Marguerite open sugar or nut cup.

29. Marguerite open sugar.

30. "Minton" mayonnaise on stand, with a hammered aluminum lid.

31. "Minton" small beaker.

32. Morning Glory salt and pepper shakers on a small tray.

33. Nantwich teacup and saucer, gilt-edged. The outside of cup, and rim of the saucer are black.

34. Old Cottage chintz plate, 6" across.

35. Pebbles bud vase. (This could also be called Bubbles.)

36. Pekin demitasse cup and saucer.

37. Pekin candy/sweets dish.

38. Peony demitasse cup and saucer.

39. Queen Anne breakfast set.

40. "Rosalind plate," 8" across. There are pebbles (or bubbles) in the center of the plate, and a floral pattern on the rim.

41. Rose Sprig breakfast set.

42. Royalty covered butter.

43. Summertime teapot.

44. Summertime tea cup.

45. Sweet Pea cup and saucer.

45A. Victorian Rose 2-slice toast rack.

46. Winifred Tennis Set.

LUSTRE CHINTZ, P. 38
QUILTED ROSE

47. Creamer, blue.

48. Jug, 5½" high, blue.

49. Open sugar, blue.

50. Covered candy, 7" high, blue.

51. Covered jam pot, blue.

52. Demitasse cup and saucer, blue.

53. Cup, blue, with Rosebud handle.

54. Teacup and saucer, pink with Rosebud handle.

55. Basket, pink.

56. Covered sugar with Rosebud finial, cranberry.

57. Creamer with Rosebud handle, cranberry.

BROCADE

58. Covered jam pot, with no underliner. Cranberry, with gold finial.

COMMEMORATIVE AND PATRIOTIC WARE, PP. 39–40

59. WWI plate, 7¾" across, with Bairnsfather cartoon. Embossed on the plate are "Coiffure in the Trenches" and "Keep yer head still, or I'll 'ave yer blinkin' ear off." Wedgewood-type plate rim. Backstamp reads "Souvenir of the Great War. Commenced Aug 4th 1914. Armistice Nov 11th 1918. Sole Makers Grimwades Ltd. Stoke on Trent." Rare.

60. WWII teacup and saucer. President Franklin D. Roosevelt and Prime Minister Winston Churchill are pictured on both cup and saucer. Rare.

61. WWI plate, 7¾" across. Bairnsfather cartoon of Old Bill with can of plum and apple preserves. Underneath the cartoon is "When the 'ell is it goin' to be strawberry?" Back of plate has holes for hanging. Marked "Made by the Girls of Staffordshire During the Winter of 1917/18 When the 'Boys' Were in the Trenches Fighting for Liberty and Civilization." Rare.

The following Churchill commemorative pieces, all white and identically marked with a navy blue flag and the red letter "D", were probably made to recognize a series of Canadian visits on the dates marked. One also commemorates a visit by the then Duke of Edinburgh (Prince Philip).

62. Ash tray marked "Churchill August 1951."

63. Ash tray marked "Churchill August 1951."

64. Covered box. The top has cameo and "HRH The duke of Edinburgh" embossed on the front, and "Churchill July 1954" on the side.

65. Oval box marked "Churchill July 1965."

66. Covered box marked "Churchill July 1952."

67. Candlestick holder. "Churchill July 1958."

68. Jug, 3½" high marked "Churchill July 1955."

69. Compote with pedestal, 7" across. Marked "To Commemorate the Visit of Their Majesties King George VI and Queen Elizabeth to Canada and the United States of America 1939."

70. Plate, 9" across with embossed Wedgewood-type rim. Marked "Queen Elizabeth II Crowned June 2 1953."

71. Plate, 7" across in blue, marked "Canada." Has British and American flags crossed over Canadian flag, c. 1938.

72. Candy or sweets dish, 5½" across. Marked on back "Hearts of Oak" "Canada 1955." On the front "Nelson's Victory 1805."

73. Candy or sweets dish, marked "Elizabeth II Crowned June 2 1953."

74. Small mug marked "George V" "Queen Mary" and "Long May They Reign Crowned June 22nd 1911."

75. Mug depicting Queen Elizabeth, marked "Crowned June 2 1953."

76. Mug marked "Queen Elizabeth, King George VI" and "Coronation May 12th 1937."

77. Mug picturing Admiral Beatty and General Haig, marked "For Freedom and Honour" and "Peace 1919."

78. Mug depicting Queen Mary and King George V. "Silver Jubilee 1910–1935" is on the front.

79. Teacup and saucer with "Queen Elizabeth II Crowned June 2 1953."

80. Mug marked "HM Queen Mary HM King George V" and "Silver Jubilee 1910–1935."

81. Teacup and saucer marked "Queen Elizabeth II Crowned June 2 1953."

COTTAGE WARE, PP. 41–42

This category includes Olde England, Ye Olde Inne, Ye Olde Mill, Beehive, Pixie, Chanticleer (or Rooster) and Lakeland pieces. Some are marked Royal Winton, others have no backstamps, some say "Made in England." Colorings are strikingly different from other makers' cottage ware. Markings shown on each piece are in quotations.

82. Plate, 8¾" across. Marked "Olde England Hand Painted" on the bottom, and depicting Anne Hathaway's Cottage.

83. Plate, 8¾" across. Marked "Ye Olde Inne Hand Painted" on the bottom. There is a sign picturing a swan in front of the pub..

84. Plate, 8¾" across. Marked "Olde England Hand Painted" on the bottom, and depicting a cottage.

85. Biscuit barrel with raffia handle. Ye Olde Mill with a red roof, marked "Made in England" on the bottom. Biscuit barrels were originally so called because they were shaped like barrels. What the British call biscuits, Americans call cookies, which are stored in cookie jars.

86. Biscuit barrel with raffia handle, yellow roof. Marked "Rubian Ware" and "Olde England Hand Painted" on the bottom.

87. Biscuit barrel with raffia handle. In a beehive shape, marked "Beehive."

88. Cream jug marked "Made in England."

89. Sugar marked "Made in England."

90. Hot water jug marked "Made in England."

91. Teapot with a red roof, marked "Ye Olde Inne."

92. Plate, 8¾" across. Lakeland.

93. Four-slice toast rack, Lakeland. Has the Royal Winton circular trademark, and stamped "Regd. No. 810586" (not entirely clear).

94. Divided relish, marked "Lakeland."

95. Teapot, marked "Rooster Reg. No. 810178" (numbers not entirely clear).

96. Sugar Shaker, a red Pixie.

97. Covered cheese keeper, "Ye Olde Mill." Unmarked.

98. Four-piece condiment set. Marked "Olde England Hand Painted."

NOVELTY RELIEF

99. Covered cheese keeper, with a mouse for the finial.

100. Butter pot marked "Jersey." The finial is a reclining cow.

RELIEF WARE, P. 43

101. Handled open basket with green and red tomatoes, and blossoms in relief. 12¹/₂" across.

102. Vegetable bowl, 11¹/₂" across. Leafy green, with onions, pea pods, radishes, turnips and onions in relief.

103. Long, leaf-shaped dish, 11" from edge to edge.

104. Long, leaf-shaped dish, 11" from edge to edge.

105. Long, leaf-shaped dish with tomatoes, 13" edge to edge.

106. Rhubarb dish, 14" from edge to edge. Has streaks of yellow and rhubarb pink, and leafy ends.

107. Tall lily vase, with one stem forming the handle.

108. Mint sauce boat with underliner. Green with pink blossoms, and pea pods forming the handle.

109. Rhubarb dish with streaks of yellow and pink, and leafy ends. 13" from edge to edge.

HANDPAINTED, PP. 44–46

Transferware that is merely enhanced or embellished by some hand painting has not been included in this section. Red Roof pieces are included because they are consistently hand-painted, and are so sought after.

110. Vase, 8¹/₂" high, with black stripes and a band of flowers. "Tiber" pattern, pictured in the 1913 catalog. Has the 1906 backstamp.

111. Fruit bowl, 10¹/₂" across. Flowers in autumn colors outlined in gilt, on a light green, bubble background. There are flowers inside and outside of the bowl.

112. Jug, 9¹/₂" high. Pink roses and dark green leaves on white lustre.

113. Biscuit barrel with chrome handle, rim and lid.

114. Footed compote, 7" across. Anemone pattern.

115. Bowl with chrome rim, floral on lustre background. The inside edge measures 6" across.

116. Cake stand, 6" across on a chrome base. Lily pattern.

117. Rectangular bowl, 9³/₄" across. Floral bouquet on orange lustre.

118. Plate, 9" across. Autumn flowers and dark green leaves on a pale orange, bubbly background. Has a gilded edge and deep magenta accents.

119. Jug, 6¹/₂" high, enameled. Oriental design that is heavily gilded, marked "Rubian Art."

120. Jug, 8" high, enameled. Oriental design that is heavily gilded, marked "Rubian Art."

121. Rectangular compote on metal stand. A blonde fairy perches in a cherry tree against a cobalt blue night sky. There are cherry blossoms around a gilded edge. Unmarked.

122. Jardiniere, blue, with floral band around the top. Marked "Rubian Art."

123. Jug, 6¹/₂" high, Art Deco floral design. Has gilded edge and sun rays with orange accents on a white lustre.

124. Jam pot with underliner. It should have a chrome lid. Marked "Fairy Castles."

125. Jam pot with underliner. This also should have a chrome lid. It is in a squashed shape, with a spider web and touches of red enamel.

There are several patterns that feature red roofs. These are transfer pieces, in different shapes and designs, with varying amounts of hand painting added. All of them are appealing, and popular with collectors.

126. Plate, 10" across. Red roof house with pond and flowers, gilt-edged.

127. Pin dish or ash tray, 4½" across. Red roof house with pond and flowers.

128. Plate, 9" across, with gilded edge. Red roof house on a road, with pond and ducks.

129. Plate, 7" across, with gilded edge. Red roof house with pond and flowers.

130. Plate, 7" across, with gilded edge. Red roof house with pond and flowers.

131. Cup and saucer. Red roof house with pond and flowers.

132. Small bowl. Red roof house with pond and flowers.

133. Candy or sweets bowl. Red roof "Old English Manor House." Delphinium garden design.

134. Pin tray. Red roof "Old English Manor House." Delphinium garden design.

135. Demitasse cup and saucer. Red roof house with pond and garden.

HOUSEHOLD WARE, PP. 47–48

Information in quotation marks is printed directly on the piece.

136. Foot warmer. Marked "the Mecca Hot Water Bottle" and "RD. NO. 474756." These were consistently manufactured since their invention. They warm equally well in the cold bed of a humble cottage or a drafty castle. The warmer pictured here has a 1945 backstamp.

137. The "Quick-Cooker Bowl," marked "Pat. No. 15043109 1261." Grimwades promoted their wares with advertising on the piece itself. The inside, front and lid all have detailed instructions on their use. The underside of the lid advertises and illustrates four other Grimwade products: "Patent Fly Proof Milk Jug Saves Child Life" is one. Another reads "The Grimwade Patent Pie Dish, grooved at bottom with vents for air passage like this [arrow points to illustration] to prevent burning at bottom." The third reads "The Grimwade Hygienic Mug, non splash top. Unchippable edge. Perfect pourer. No sharp edges on inside

to hold dirt." And, "The Grimwade Safety Milk Bowl (9 sizes). For keeping out flies." Lastly, there is a reminder to "ask at any china store for these articles."

138. Oval drainer, 7½" x 5" across. Marked with "The Grimwades Patent Hygienic Convex Flutes Drainer. Bevel edge holes."

139. Round drainer, 4" across. Unmarked.

140. Round drainer, 5¾" across. Marked "The Grimwades Patent Hygienic Convex Flutes Drainer. Bevel edge holes."

141. Inhaler, 8" high with the 1945 backstamp. Marked "Dr. Nelson's Improved Inhaler." Clear and concise directions for its use are printed on the piece. This was another invention produced continuously throughout the years.

142. Pie Vent (also called a Pie Bird on account of the whistling noise it made as it released steam while baking).

143. Humidor, with original rubber seal, original brass closer and 1951 backstamp. Transfer design of a village/cottage scene. These were used to keep cigars moist, different from tobacco jars which were used to keep pipe tobacco moist. Humidors had a sealed top, whereas tobacco jars had only a lid. A must for the man of the house, when smoking was considered an expected after-dinner pleasure.

144. Lemon squeezer, 7" across, c. 1945.

145. Wash basin, 16½" across. Marked "Wisteria" and "Rd No 484760" c. 1900.

146. Bed pan marked "Perfection Bed and Douche Pan" and "The most sanitary and comfortable bed pan in the world. For Hospital and Home."

147. Slipper-shaped bed pan, marked "The New Slipper Bed Pan."

148. Chamber pot, 8¾" across. Marked "Festoon Border."

149. Chamber pot, 9¼" across. Marked "Flaxman" and has a pre-1900 backstamp.

LEAF WARE, PP. 49–50

Various items were made in the shape of a maple leaf, and in a variety of colors. Because the maple leaf is Canada's national symbol, and because this pattern is found in abundance in Canada but is scarce elsewhere, it seems logical to assume that it was made for export to Canada. Leaf ware is usually found in shades of cream, brown, green, pink and orange. Some pieces are gilded.

150. Candy dish, 8¹/₄" across. Golden Age finish applied to the top.

151. Compote, pale orange and green, metal base.

152. Candy dish, 8³/₄" across. Golden Age finish applied to the top.

153. Creamer and sugar, pale green.

154. Long salad dish, 10¹/₂" across. Green with gilded leaf veins.

155. Creamer and sugar. Pale orange and green.

156. Serving knife in pale orange and green.

157. Four-slice toast rack.

158. Cake plate with chrome handle. Brown and green.

159. Jam pot with lid.

160. Two-tiered cake plate, chrome handle.

161. Two-tiered cake plate, chrome handle.

162. Handled candy or sweets dish with chrome handle.

163. Serving dish, 9" across.

164. Serving dish, 8" across.

165. Creamer and sugar on tray. Golden Age outside of the creamer and sugar. Pink inside the creamer and sugar and tray. Gilded edge.

166. Creamer and sugar on tray. Pink with gilded edges.

167. Creamer and sugar on tray. Golden Age inside of pieces with gilded handles.

LUSTRE WARE, PP. 51–54

Lustre ware comes in varying shades and multiple colors, sometimes with a transfer design, and often with hand painting as well.

168. Two-tiered cake plate with chrome handle. Blue.

169. Basket, with a handpainted lily design.

170. Three-tier cake plate with chrome handle.

171. Tennis set.

172. Tennis set, multi-color lustre.

173. Creamer and sugar.

174. Open handled candy dish.

175. Teapot, stacked.

176. Creamer and sugar.

177. Basket.

178. Three-tier cake plate. Chrome handle, Art Deco design.

179. Candy or sweets dish with striped design.

180. Salad bowl with silver rim and striped design.

181. Wall pocket.

182. Wall pocket in Art Deco design.

183. Covered box.

184. Covered butter.

185. Jam pot with lid, square.

SHAKESPEARE SERIES
The following three pieces all have an illustration of a Shakespeare character.

186. Long dish, 11" across. Marked "Shakespeare Series Grimwades England" and "Orlando."

187. Jug, 5³/₄" high. Marked "Shakespeare Series Grimwades England" and "Rosalind, Celia and Touchstone."

188. Teapot, 6-cup. Marked "Shakespeare Series Grimwades England" and "Orlando."

189. Salad Bowl, 10¹/₂" across, with pair of servers. White lustre.

190. Small creamer with tiny pink roses. Has a Baleek look.

191. Sugar and creamer with shell handle. Has a Baleek look.

192. Teapot, 6-cup, with shell finial. Baleek look.

193. Long dish, 11" from edge to edge. Ribbed.

194. Fruit bowl, 10" across. Art Deco design.

195. Long, rectangular dish. 10" from edge to edge.

196. Long, rectangular dish. 10" from edge to edge.

The teacups and saucers listed below show the variety of Royal Winton's lustre shapes and color.

197. Teacup and saucer.

198. Teacup and saucer.

199. Teacup and saucer.

200. Sundae dish with attached base.

201. Teacup and saucer.

202. Teacup and saucer. One might find these at garage or estate sales. Saucers are handy as underliners for glass sherbets; small open sugars can be used as nut cups.

203. Teacup and saucer.

204. Teacup and saucer.

205. Demitasse cup and saucer.

206. Teacup and saucer.

Golden and Silver Age, pp. 55–56

The undersides of these pieces are white, to minimize signs of wear. Colors are frequently mingled—gold on the outside, silver on the inside or vice-versa.

207. Basket, gold.

208. Handled tray, 10½" across. Gold.

209. Open handled dish with a painted lily.

210. Bud vase, 6" high. Gold.

211. Teacup and saucer. Silver, with the inside of the cup gold.

212. Teapot, 6-cup. Silver.

213. Footed compote, 7½" across. Gold.

214. Square covered butter. Silver with gold finial.

215. Teacup and Saucer, silver. The inside of the cup is gold.

216. Jam pot with lid. Gold, white on the inside.

217. Creamer and sugar on tray. Silver. There is gold inside the creamer and sugar.

218. Vase with insert for flower display. 5¾" high, gold.

219. Teacup and saucer, gold.

220. Teapot, 6-cup. Gold.

221. Vase, 4½" across the top. Gold.

222. Teacup and saucer. Gold floral design.

223. Teacup and saucer. Gold.

224. Teacup and saucer. The cup is gold with a handpainted floral design inside. Signed by the artist.

225. Demitasse cup and saucer. Gold.

226. Teacup and saucer, gold.

227. Creamer and sugar on tray. Molded design on tray ends.

228. Creamer and sugar on tray. Gold.

Mottled Ware, p. 57

229. Footed fruit bowl in green with gilded edge.

230. Tray, possibly for holding creamer and sugar. Pink.

231. Candy or sweets dish. Yellow with gold Art Deco trim.

232. Tray, possibly for holding creamer and sugar. Green.

233. Candy or sweets dish. Pink.

234. Creamer and covered sugar. Green with Rosebud finial.

235. Demitasse cup and saucer. Rouge with gilded edges and handle.

236. Stacked teapot. Rouge with gilded edges, handles and finial.

237. Four-slice toast rack. Green.

238. Saville Toast and Marmalade. Pink.

239. Tray, possibly for holding creamer and sugar. Yellow.

240. Square covered butter. Green.

241. Compote on pedestal. Rouge with gilded edge.

242. Breakfast set, green.

243. Three-part divided relish. Gilded edge.

MUGS AND JUGS, P. 58

244. Musical beer mug. There is a mountain lake scene with a tiny fisherman in a row boat in relief. The handle is a man wearing yellow breeches, boots and a green hunting coat, gazing pensively into the mug, which plays "How Dry I Am."

245. Beer mug. Villagers dancing on the green are depicted in relief. Bottom of the handle is a violin, the top is a set of bagpipes. This mug is not musical, but could be made so with a mechanical unit.

246. Musical beer mug. Village scene of horse and buggy. Plays "I Love to Go a'Wandering."

247. Fish-shaped gurgling mug, 9" high. The open mouth is the spout, and the tail curves into a hollow handle. Makes a gurgling sound when poured.

CHARACTER MUGS

These are wonderfully realistic portraits of the figures they portray, with handles that are appropriate for each piece.

248. Uncle Sam. His tall grey top hat has a blue band with white stars. Wears a high stiff collar, a tan and brown cravat tied in a bow, and a grim expression. His hair covers the collar in back. Bushy eyebrows and pointed grey beard. The mug's handle is formed of tan and brown dollar signs. Large, 7$^1/_2$" high.

249. General Sir Archibald Wavell, looking serious and wearing a frown. His khaki uniform and hat have insignia and braid in detail. The mug's handle is a sword. Medium size, 6$^1/_2$" high.

250. King Henry VIII. Plain handle, undecorated. Medium size, 5$^3/_4$" high. Proportionally, this mug is wider and fatter ("larger than life") than most medium mugs. It has been classified as medium size because of its height.

251. King George VI is depicted in black military uniform, with proper insignia. The braided handle resembles the handle of a ceremonial sword. Small size, 3$^3/_4$" high.

252. Uncle Sam mug, in smaller size 4$^3/_4$" high. Same grey top hat and blue band with stars, but his cravat is a reddish brown, and the handle is formed of green and brown dollar signs.

253. President Franklin D. Roosevelt, hatless. He is wearing a dark pinstripe suit and a white shirt. The knot of a maroon necktie shows. Teeth showing slightly. Small size, 4" high.

254. General Sir Archibald Wavell. Same detail as larger mug, but with more color on face. Serious, frowning expression. Miniature size, 3" high.

255. King George VI. Cream-colored, undecorated. Miniature size, 2$^3/_4$" high.

256. "Canadian Mountie" in red uniform, with a khaki hat. Blue and yellow epaulets on the shoulders, blue and yellow at the throat, and a white cord around the neck. The handle to this mug has a set of spurs at the top and bottom.

257. King George VI. Same detail as in the larger mugs. Miniature size, 2$^1/_2$" high.

NURSERY WARE, P. 59

Grimwades/Royal Winton made a large number of nursery pieces. But today these pieces are scarce, probably because they were used by children on a daily basis, and vulnerable to breakage.

258. Bowl, double wall. 6$^3/_4$" across, with a coaching scene on the inside. Has a 1930 backstamp.

259. Bowl, double wall. 6³/₄" across, marked "Dickens Souvenir." Charles Dickens scene on the inside of the bowl.

260. Mug with "Pip the Panda" illustration.

261. Mug marked "Dickens Souvenir." Dickens character Captain Cuttle is on one side, with Mr. Pickwick on the other.

Pastel Ware, p. 60

Pastel ware is pale but vibrant, and comes in cream, pink, green or yellow. Rosebud, mottled ware and some molded relief pieces come in these same colors. However mottled ware also includes a deeper rouge tone. The mottled pieces shown here represent the contrast of pastel colors.

262. Plate, 8" across. Pink.

263. Plate, 7" across. Cream.

264. Fruit bowl, 9" across. Pink with a yellow design.

265. Watercress bowls, 10" across. The top bowl is slightly smaller, with holes to drain newly washed watercress. Molded relief edge. Yellow.

266. Candy or sweets bowl, 7" across. Rounded triangular shape. Green with gilded edge.

267. Plate, 8" across. Pink with gilded edge.

268. Sundae dish with attached base. Orange/tan.

269. Candy or sweets dish, 7¹/₂" across. Yellow with black on the handles.

270. Open sugar or nut dish. Green with gilded edge.

271. Long candy or sweets dish, 6¹/₂" across. Open handles, yellow.

272. Covered box. Cream with gilded edge.

273. Square plate, 8". Yellow with gilded edge.

274. Square plate, 7". Yellow with gilded edge.

275. Square plate, 8". Green with gilded edge.

Pastel/Molded Relief, pp. 61–62

276. Creamer and sugar. Pink with Fuchsia design.

277. Creamer and sugar on tray. Pink with cherries in relief.

278. Bud vase. Green with gilded edge.

279. Bud vase. Yellow with gilded edge.

280. Mint or sauce boat with underliner. Fuchsia.

281. Teacup and saucer. Mottled, rouge color with gilded handle.

282. Wall pocket. Yellow with gilded trim.

283. Covered butter with gilded finial. Mottled, rouge color.

284. Two-slice toast rack. Green with gilded edge.

285. Creamer and sugar. Mottled, green color.

286. Creamer and sugar. Yellow with gilded edge.

287. Creamer and sugar. Mottled, rouge color with gilded trim.

288. Fruit bowl, marked "Golden Rhapsody." White with gilded outline of rose.

289. Candy or sweets dish. White with gold design.

290. Long dish, 13" from edge to edge. Marked "Golden Rhapsody." White with gilded outline of a rose.

291. Dish, 6¹/₂" across. With brass handle and gilded edge.

292. Long dish, 13" from edge to edge. Green with pink lily.

293. Footed compote, 6" high. Pink with silver leaves.

294. Wall clock (it works). Yellow and pink, with the original wind-up key.

295. Long dish, 13" from edge to edge. Pink with pink lily.

296. Candy or sweets dish. 13" long. Pink with gilded edge. Heraldic design.

297. Tennis set. Blue with a gilded fuchsia.

298. Handled cake plate. White with green leaves and a pink daisy-like flower.

299. Handled cake plate. Pink with gilded edge.

ROSEBUD/MOLDED RELIEF, PP. 63–66

This category includes the Fuchsia, Petunia, Tiger Lily and Rosebud designs.

300. Tray, Rosebud pattern in pink.

301. Bowl, Tiger Lily pattern in green.

302. Tray, Tiger Lily pattern in yellow.

303. Tray or sauce underliner. Tiger Lily pattern in green.

304. Teapot, 6 cup. Cream with Rosebud top and handle.

305. Trivet, cream.

306. Tennis set. Fuchsia design in pink.

307. Salt and pepper on a tray. Rosebud pattern in yellow, green and pink.

308. Two-slice toast rack. Green, with a primrose design in relief.

309. Creamer and sugar on tray. Rosebud design in yellow.

310. Condiment set with wood and metal handles. Green, yellow and pink.

311. Teacup and saucer. Cream, with Fuchsia on handle.

312. Milk jug. Pink with peaches in relief.

313. Fruit bowl, 9" across. Yellow with floral handles.

314. Jug with lid. Floral design with Rosebud finial. Green.

315. Teacup and saucer, green. Rosebud handle.

316. Footed compote. Pink with floral relief and gilded edges.

317. Tennis set. Yellow Rosebud.

318. Condiment set on tray. Green with gilded rim.

319. Mint or sauce boat and tray. Yellow Tiger Lily.

320. Jam or marmalade dish with knife and spoon. Primrose design. Green.

321. Salt and pepper shakers with Rosebud. Pink and yellow.

322. Two-slice toast rack. Tiger Lily.

323. Trio, consisting of teacup, saucer and 7" plate. Pink with Petunia handle.

324. Tennis set. Petunia design. Yellow.

325. Candy or sweets dish. Petunia design. Yellow.

326. Four-slice toast rack. Cream with gilded edge.

327. Demitasse cup and saucer. Green with Rosebud handle.

328. Teacup and saucer. Pink with petunia handle.

329. Four-slice toast rack. Tiger lily design. Green.

330. Divided candy or sweets dish. Primrose. Cream with pink edge.

331. Four-slice toast rack. Floral design. Green.

332. Candy or sweets dish. Primrose design. Cream.

333. Open sugar or nut cup. Green with gilded edge.

334. Candlestick holder. Green, decorated with a pink rosebud.

335. Cream jug. Tiger Lily design. Cream with green edge.

336. Fruit bowl, 10" across. Footed, pink with yellow flowers.

337. Coffee pot with lid. Cream with Rosebud finial and handle.

338. Candy or sweets dish. Green with leafy edges.

339. Covered trinket holder. Green with Rosebud finial.

340. Three-tier cake plate, each plate a different color. Open rose design.

341. Candy or sweets dish. Green.

342. Four-slice toast rack. Green with Rosebud handle.

343. Jam Pot. Green with gilded edge and Rosebud finial.

344. Creamer. Green with Rosebud handle.

345. Candlestick holder. Rosebud design. Green.

346. Candlestick holder. Rosebud design. Green.

347. Condiment set. Rosebud design, in pink and yellow.

SOUVENIR WARE, PP. 67–73

These are usually easy-to-pack items to carry home as gifts or reminders of a memorable vacation. Royal Winton pieces can be found from popular or historical vacation destinations in Britain, Canada and the United States. Heraldic pieces—designed with city crests—came from Canada or Scotland.

348. Creamer and Sugar. Heraldic, cream.

349. Creamer and Sugar. Heraldic, blue.

350. Plate, 9" across. Heraldic, blue.

351. Creamer and Sugar. Heraldic, yellow.

352. Teacup and saucer. Heraldic, cream.

353. Teacup and saucer. Heraldic, cream.

354. Teapot, 6-cup. Heraldic, cream.

355. Creamer. Heraldic, cream.

356. Salt and pepper on tray. Heraldic, yellow.

357. Covered box. Heraldic, cream.

358. Cream jug. Heraldic, cream with gilded edge.

359. Tray. Heraldic, cream.

360. Open sugar or nut cup. Heraldic, cream with gilded edge.

361. Plate, 10¹/₂" across. Depicting "Le Vieux Canada," or "Old Canada," and dated 1953. Gilded edge.

362. Toothpick. Depicting "Le Vieux Canada," or "Old Canada," and dated 1953.

363. Tray, 9¹/₂" across. Depicting "Le Vieux Canada" or "Old Canada," and dated 1953. Gilded edge.

364. Handled tray. Gilded edge. Showing a "Georgian Tavern 1750."

365. Triangular tray, 10¹/₄" from edge to edge. Depicting scenes of "Le Vieux Canada" or "Old Canada," and dated 1953. Gilded edge.

366. Toothpick (or 3-handled cup) marked "Atlas Heraldic China. C.R. & C.S." and "Old Glasgow Scottish Exhibition 1911."

367. Post-WWII mug with red enameled flowers. Depicting "La Villa Gardens Bermuda."

368. Creamer marked "Cornish Scenes" and "Lands End." There is a sailboat pictured on one side.

369. Teacup and saucer, depicting "Friday Becomes Crusoe's Slave."

370. Demitasse cup and saucer depicting "An Old Bermuda Home." Red enamel flowers.

371. Demitasse cup and saucer depicting "An Ancient Buttery" and marked "Bermuda."

U. S. souvenir pieces have a Jon Roth backstamp in addition to the Royal Winton mark. Similar pieces are shown to indicate the variety of shapes and sizes in the same item.

372. Plate, 10" across. On the front is "Rock City Garden Mountain." Marked "Imported exclusively for beautiful Rock City Gardens on top of Historic Lookout Mountain." Jon Roth backstamp.

373. Ash tray, 4¹/₂" across. "First Berry-Lincoln Store and Post Office" on the front; "Lincoln's New Salem, Illinois" on the back. Jon Roth backstamp.

374. Teacup and saucer. Depicting "Lincoln's Home Springfield Illinois." Jon Roth backstamp.

375. Small teapot depicting "Old Faithful Geyser, Yellowstone Park." Jon Roth backstamp.

376. Demitasse teacup and saucer with "Governor's House, Williamsburg, Virginia." Jon Roth backstamp.

377. Teacup and saucer. Depicting "Old Faithful Geyser, Yellowstone Park." Jon Roth backstamp.

378. Creamer and sugar. Depicting "Old Faithful Geyser, Yellowstone National Park." Jon Roth backstamp. Different in shape than (377), but shown as a set. Same illustration.

379. Creamer and sugar. Depicting "Governor's House, Williamsburg, Virginia." Jon Roth backstamp.

Niagara Falls, a popular honeymoon spot that borders New York and Ontario, Canada, is pictured on souvenir ware from both the Canadian and the U. S. sides. Since all pieces found carry the Royal Winton mark, it is assumed that the place depicted is in Canada, unless it also carries the Jon Roth backstamp.

380. Handled mint or sweets dish. Depicting "General View, Niagara Falls, Canada."

381. Creamer and sugar. Depicting "Prospect Point, Niagara Falls."

382. Creamer depicting "General View, Niagara Falls."

383. Teacup and saucer. Depicting "General View, Niagara Falls."

384. Salt and peppers. Showing "Little White House, Warm Springs, Georgia." Jon Roth backstamp.

385. Open sugar depicting "Prospect Point, Niagara Falls."

386. Creamer depicting "General View, Niagara Falls."

387. Small creamer with "Prospect Point, Niagara Falls."

388. Sugar depicting "Mt Edith Cavell Jasper Park."

389. Creamer with "Lions Gate Bridge from Prospect Point, Vancouver B. C."

390. Beaker, 4" high showing "Mt Edith Cavell Jasper Park."

391. Jug, 4¹/₂" high showing "Villa de Quebec Quebec City."

392. Creamer and sugar with "Old St. Louis Gate Quebec."

393. Creamer and sugar with "Chateau Frontenac, Quebec, Canada."

394. Jug, 4¹/₂" high showing "Perce Rock, Perce Que."

395. Creamer and sugar with "Indian Totem Poles, Thunderbird Park. Victoria B. C., Canada."

396. Plate, 6" across, showing "Mt Athabasca, Columbia Ice Field From the Jasper-Banff Highway."

397. Plate, 5" across, with "Indian Racing Canoe, Chemainus B. C."

398. Footed compote, 5" across. Depicting "Administration Building, Ontario Agricultural College."

399. Plate, 6¹/₂" across. Marked "Home of Anne of Green Gables. National Park P. E. I."

400. Teacup and saucer with "Mt Rundle, Banff."

401. Teacup and saucer showing "Casa Loma Toronto, Canada."

402. Teacup and saucer with "The Lions, Vancouver B. C."

403. Candy or sweets dish with open handle, 7" across. Marked "Sherridon, Man."

404. Covered box depicting "Banff and Mt Cascade From Administration Building."

405. Teacup and saucer. Depicting "Grand Canyon." Jon Roth backstamp.

406. Ash tray or mint dish. Depicting "Grand Canyon National Park, Arizona." Jon Roth backstamp.

407. Shell-shaped nut or pin dish. Depicting "Grand Canyon." Jon Roth backstamp.

408. Teacup and saucer. Marked "Grand Canyon." Jon Roth backstamp.

409. Demitasse cup and saucer. Depicting "Grand Canyon National Park, Arizona." Jon Roth backstamp.

410. Demitasse cup and saucer, with "Washington's Headquarters, Valley Forge, VA." Jon Roth backstamp.

411. Tray, 8" across. Gilded edge. Shows "Half Dome, Yosemite National Park, California." Jon Roth backstamp.

412. Pin dish, 3³/₄" across. Shows "Half Dome, Yosemite National Park, California." Jon Roth backstamp.

413. Small teapot. Depicting "Half Dome, Yosemite National Park, California." Jon Roth backstamp.

414. Demitasse cup and saucer. Marked "Half

Dome, Yosemite National Park, California." Jon Roth backstamp.

415. Open sugar or nut cup. Depicting "Cliff House and Seal Rocks, San Francisco, California." Jon Roth backstamp.

416. Demitasse cup. Depicting "Cliff House and Seal Rocks, San Francisco, California." Jon Roth backstamp.

417. Plate, 5" across, with "Bennington National Monument. Bennington Vt." Jon Roth backstamp.

418. Creamer depicting "The Temple. Salt Lake City, Utah." Jon Roth backstamp.

419. Salt and pepper shakers, with "Bolt Castle, 1000 Islands. Alexandria Bay, NY." Jon Roth backstamp.

420. Demitasse cup and saucer. Depicting "The Flume Gorge, Franconium Notch, New Hampshire." Jon Roth backstamp.

421. Teacup and saucer. Depicting "The Temple. Salt Lake City, Utah." Jon Roth backstamp.

British historical events, costumes, and places were depicted on some pieces. Transfer patterns. Most are handpainted and gilt-edged. Many were made for export, with dates and registry numbers listed for Canada and Australia.

422. Footed compote, 6¹/₂" across. Has costumed figures, and is marked "Gainsborough Can. Reg. 1954."

423. Divided relish dish, 9" across. Village scenes.

424. Open-handled tray, 10³/₄" across. Marked "Old English Markets. CAN RD. 1952. AUS. RD. 29636."

425. Pin dish or ash tray. Handpainted, marked "Happy Days."

426. Rectangular tray, 10" across. Marked "Old English Markets. CAN RD. 1952. AUS. RD. 29636."

427. Candy or sweets dish, 7" across. Marked "Royal Scenes. William I at the Tower 1075."

428. Teacup and saucer. With "Mediaeval Ale House 1450."

429. Pin tray depicting "Old London" and "St James Palace."

430. Pin tray marked "Old London" and "Cheapside."

431. Pin tray marked "Happy Days."

432. Pin tray marked "Old London" and "Temple Bar."

433. Pin tray marked Old London" and "Chelsea."

434. Pin tray marked "Happy Days."

435. Square plate, 9". Wedgewood style embossed rim. Depicting "Lady Dedlock" and peacock.

436. Square plate, 9" across. Wedgewood style embossed rim. Depicting lady standing looking out of tall window.

437. Round plate, 9" across. Wedgewood style embossed rim. Marked "Dickens Souvenir" and "Mr. Pickwick."

438. Tennis set. Marked "Old English Markets" and "Can. Reg. 1952 Aus. Reg. 1952 29646."

439. Jam pot with lid. Depicting a village scene.

440. Demitasse cup and saucer, with "Old English Markets." Marked "CAN. RD. 1942 AUS. RD. 29646."

441. Creamer and sugar with village scene.

442. Creamer and sugar depicting Old English Markets.

443. Covered trinket box. Depicting a castle and grounds with strolling couples.

444. Mint or sauce boat. Depicting a horse and buggy scene.

445. Covered trinket box with a tavern scene.

446. Plate, 9" across. Marked "Ann [sic] Hathaway's Cottage." Handpainted with blue edge.

TRANSFER WARE, PP. 74–79

447. Eight-sided plate, 9¹/₄" across. Roses and vines on an ivory background. Marked "Royal Hampton Ware" and "Grimwades Copyright."

448. Butter dish with grape border.

449. Tennis set. Shows fruit in autumn colors on a white background.

450. Tennis set. Shows an urn with floral bouquet on a green background.

451. Tennis set. Shows fruit in autumn colors on a white background.

452. Creamer and sugar with a lily.

453. Salt and pepper on tray with floral design.

454. Two-slice toast rack with primrose design.

455. Basket, 8" across, showing gate and garden view. Flowers in relief and leaves on the handle. Marked "Gateway."

The cheese keepers pictured here are examples of early transfer ware.

456. Cheese keeper. Pre-1900 mark.

457. Cheese keeper. Pre-1900 mark.

458. Cheese keeper. Pre-1900 mark.

459. Footed compote with gilded edges. Floral design. Pre-1900 mark.

460. Square plate, 7" across. Green, with an unusual mosaic design, enameled.

461. Demitasse cup and saucer. Marked "Lilly" on the bottom, and also has a pre-1900 mark.

462. Eight-sided plate, 5" across. White in the center with Egyptian motif on yellow rim. 1930 mark.

463. Mayonnaise jar. Vivid coral with Egyptian motif on yellow band. 1930 mark.

464. Cake plate, 8¹/₂" across. Chrome handle. Coral in the center with Egyptian motif on yellow band. 1930 mark.

465. Biscuit barrel with hammered metal lid. Coral, with Egyptian motif on yellow band. 1930 mark.

466. Cheese keeper. Marked "Venetian" and "Made in England." This piece matches bowl (467), which is marked "Grimwades." Unlike usual Royal Winton coloring.

467. "Venetian" bowl, 9¹/₂" across. Globe and Sash mark (1930s) and "Grimwades." This piece matches the cheese keeper (466). Unlike usual Royal Winton coloring.

468. Breakfast egg set in cobalt blue and gold. consists of four egg cups, salt shaker and pepper shaker on a tray. Marked "Royal Winton Ivory Ware" and "England."

469. Jug, blue with circular floral design in the center, enameled in white. It is possible to find this coloring in a variety of items such as mugs, trays, sauce boats, creamers, sugars and condiment sets.

470. Tray, 10" across. Blue with floral design enameled in white.

471. Mint or sauce boat. Blue with floral design enameled in white.

472. Mint or sauce boat. Blue with floral design enameled in white.

473. Mug, 4" high. Blue with floral design enameled in white.

474. Cake plate, 8¹/₂" across. Chrome handles. Blue with floral design enameled in white.

475. Condiment set. Blue with floral design enameled in white.

476. Teacup and saucer. Green, marked "Hunting Scenes."

477. Square plate, 8³/₄" across. With enameled flowers and gilded edges. Probably part of a tea set.

478. Plate, 8" across. Floral center and green rim.

479. Open sugar or nut cup. Green, marked "Hunting Scenes."

480. Pin tray that matches box (481). Depicts a dance scene. White with enameled silhouetted figures.

481. Covered trinket or cigarette box. Matches tray (480). Depicts a dance scene. White with enameled silhouetted figures.

482. Tray, 10" across. Lake scene.

483. Creamer. Cream-colored with an enameled bouquet.

484. Creamer with enameled delphiniums.

485. Covered trinket or cigarette box. Enameled floral bouquet on top.

486. Shell-shaped nut or mint dish. 4¼" across with enameled flowers.

487. Bowl, 6" across. Handpainted. White with gilded edge and 1930 mark.

488. Plate, 10" across. Cobalt blue with red, yellow and brown floral design on a white background. Marked "Belper" and "Royal Winton Ivory."

489. Covered cheese keeper. White with cobalt and gold trim.

490. Open sugar and creamer. Bright yellow with red, black and green enameled flowers and black branches. There is an "Atlas China" mark, with a figure holding a globe.

491. Creamer with a lake scene.

492. Two-slice toast rack.

493. Open sugar and creamer. Yellow with black branches, green and red enameled flowers.

494. Open sugar. Features a country cottage scene winding around the bottom of the piece. Has red enameled accents.

495. Covered butter. Cobalt blue branches, blue and yellow flowers.

496. Candy or sweets dish with open handles, 5½" across. Autumn leaves design.

497. Jam pot with chrome lid. Black with enameled red lily. Impressed with "Orleans" and a 1930 stamp.

498. Salt and pepper shakers on tray. Red, orange and yellow flowers with touches of black. One of many floral designs with an Oriental look.

499. Creamer and open sugar. White shades to yellow. Floral band with red and blue enameled flowers. Black around the top, gilt-edged.

500. Bowl, 8" across. Yellow with scene of meadow flowers and a fence. Matches long bowl (501) and has gilded edge.

501. Long bowl, 10" across. Art Deco shape, green with gilded edge. Scene of meadow flowers and fence. Matches (500), but different color.

502. Creamer and open sugar, 4½" across. With pastel flowers and green and blue bands.

503. Plate, 5" across. Handpainted. Green center with a floral design and gilded edge.

504. Candy or sweets dish. Handpainted. Roses in center with gilded edge.

505. Plate, 5" across. Green with a yellow center. Marked "Rosa" underneath.

506. Four-slice toast rack. Pink with a bare branches design.

507. Candy or sweets dish, 5½" across. Open handles. Floral design around the inside edge.

508. Open sugar or nut cup. Green with floral spray.

509. Open sugar. Orange, yellow and red with floral display. Gilded edge.

510. Stacking creamer and sugar with lid. Has deep pink primroses, with gilded edge and handle. Possibly part of stacking teapot.

TRANSFER WARE DINNER SET, P. 80

This is an example of one of Royal Winton's transfer ware dinner sets, with complete service for eight. There is no pattern name on any of the pieces. The backstamp on the set is Grimwade's circular mark, used from 1934 onward. The china is cream-colored with a floral pattern—an urn of daisy-like pink and yellow flowers—with two sprays of the same flowers on the rim of each piece. Banded in pink and green; gilt-edged.

511. Plate, 6" across.

512. Meat platter.

513. Plate, 8" across.

514. Plate, 9" across.

515. Sauce dish.

516. Open serving bowl, 9" across.

517. Waste bowl.

518. Covered serving bowl, 10" across.

519. Teacup and saucer.

520. Creamer and covered sugar.

521. Cereal bowl, 6½" across.

CHAPTER FIVE

TIPS ON CERAMIC CARE

If you display a plate by hanging it, use metal plate hangers carefully. Some exert unnecessary pressure that can weaken, damage or mark a piece. To avoid the possibility of rust marks, make sure the plate is dry before inserting it in the metal hanger. To store ceramic plates, try using paper doilies between them. This looks attractive and will protect them, especially those with gilding.

To clean old ceramics, never use strong chlorine bleach. Do not scrub with scouring powder; instead, wash them in warm, sudsy water using mild soap with a little ammonia added. Rinse and dry.

To clean stained teapots, first fill the pot with hot water. Then add a dental cleaning tablet such as Efferdent or Polident, and let it stand several hours or overnight. This method can also serve to lighten dark crazing marks (fine cracks that appear over time in a glazed surface). For cleaning other stained pieces, let them stand in a basin of hot water with a dental or Alka Seltzer tablet. Then, rinse and dry. To dry hard-to-reach areas, use a blow dryer set on warm or cool air.

Some older methods include dissolving an Alka Seltzer tablet in water, and letting the piece soak overnight. Or, combining one pint of vinegar with four pints of water, and letting the piece soak overnight.

To get at stubborn stains, try rubbing with toothpaste, then let the piece stand several hours. Rinse and dry. Or, rub damp soda on the stain. Let stand several hours, then rinse and dry. These methods can also be used on areas inside a spout or around the handle.

Another way to eliminate stains is to rub lemon juice, salted vinegar, or a mixture of $1/2$ cup ammonia and $1/2$ cup white vinegar on the stain. For really stubborn stains, beauty supply strength ammonia

(30–40%) works. It can be purchased in quantity, and reused if kept sealed. Pour ammonia, full strength, into a covered plastic container (such as Tupperware). Immerse items in it; cover, and leave up to two weeks. This works very well without damaging the item. Wear rubber gloves to avoid burns. Be sure to rinse and dry pieces thoroughly after treatment. Unfortunately, there is no sure-fire cleaning method.

For repairing broken pieces, use glue that clearly states it will repair china. Follow the directions on the container. Carefully remove excess glue with nail polish remover on a cloth or Q-Tip. Rinse and dry. To repair small chips, find a porcelain repair product which comes in shades of white, ivory or almond. A dab should cover a small chipped spot, and dry solidly enough to sand lightly in 24 hours.

The care and repair of dishes is a valid household concern. A cookbook from the mid-1800s contained "useful receipts for housekeepers and servants," including how to repair broken china. It reads:

TO CEMENT BROKEN CHINA—
Beat lime to a very fine, almost invisible dust, sift it through book muslin. Then tie it up in a piece of thin muslin as powdered starch is sometimes used. Brush some white of egg over the edges of china, dust the lime rapidly over them, put the edges together, and tie a string round the cup, etc. till it is firm. Eisinglass dissolved in spirits of wine, in the proportion of one ounce to two wineglassfuls of the spirit, is also a good cement. (From *Warne's Everyday Cookery Book, Compiled by Mary Jewry With 1000 Receipts and Hints on Marketing, Ordering Dinner, Carving, Napkin Folding.*)

1913 CATALOG REPRINT

Nineteen-thirteen was an important year for Grimwades Ltd. King George V and Queen Mary visited the Potteries at Stoke-on-Trent, which had spent many months modeling, firing and decorating wares for the special occasion. Queen Mary had been particularly admiring of two Royal Winton items: the Quick-Cooker; and the Mecca Foot Warmer in Jacobean chintz.

In honor of the visit, a special catalog was printed and circulated shortly afterward. The catalog contained a short history of Grimwades Ltd., press notices from local papers alluding to the Royal visit, photographs of the potters and their displays, a list of the firm's directors and representatives, color illustrations of some of their lines, and advertisements that demonstrated the efficiency of the "Ideal" Display Blocks and other patented products.

Very few copies of this catalog are available, and I was fortunate to find one of them when I met Reg and May Bladen in England, in 1996. We have reprinted the catalog here so the reader might enjoy the information as it was originally presented, in the language of the time. The original pages 1, 2, 11, 12 and 29 had been lost or destroyed before I obtained the catalog; therefore only photocopies of these pages are shown here.

Royal Visit to the • •
Staffordshire Potteries.

GRIMWADES

GRIMWADES, Ltd.,

Winton Pottery, ✦ ✦

Stoke-on-Trent, Staffs.

IN COMMEMORATION
OF THE VISIT TO THE POTTERIES
OF THEIR MAJESTIES

King George V. and Queen Mary

ON TUESDAY, APRIL 22nd, 1913.

GRIMWADES, Ltd.,

WINTON POTTERY,

STOKE-ON-TRENT, England.

LONDON SHOW ROOM:
Winton House,
13, St. Andrew Street, E.C.

WINTON POTTERY

as decorated on the occasion of Royal Visit to Stoke-on-Trent, April 22nd, 1913.

An interesting feature was the holding of banners by Messrs. Grimwade's Potters, each one having a separate letter and the whole forming an appropriate Motto as follows:—

"No craft there is that can with ours compare,
We make our pots of what we potters are."

WINTON POTTERY, which covers nearly 2 acres, is replete with the most up-to-date Machinery, including Climax Kilns, by means of which 500,000 Mugs and Beakers were decorated and fired in the incredibly short period of 5 weeks; prior to the Coronation of King George V. and Queen Mary, in 1911.

History of the Firm.

THE business of Grimwade Bros. was founded in the year 1885, and although commenced in quite a small way, such was the initial energy with which it was started that it rapidly gained an important position in the trade. China merchants, wholesale and retail, throughout the United Kingdom welcomed the new enterprise with its up-to-date ideas, and improved methods of business

For several years in succession, the turnover *doubled every 12 months.* In 1890, an Export Department was established and soon the productions of the firm were known throughout the British Empire, and indeed throughout the civilized world. To cope with this extraordinary development of trade, the well-known and prominent Winton Pottery was built in the year 1892 with a four-story elevation and a frontage of 180 feet on the main road, and within 3 minutes walk of Stoke-on-Trent Station. The factory was built on the most approved lines and is replete with up-to-date equipment. It extends for a long distance at the rear covering in all nearly 2 acres. In subsequent years, the whole of this large area has been built up with a network of ovens, kilns and workshops, whilst from time to time, new machinery has been introduced until Winton Pottery to-day is one of the best equipped factories in the world.

In March 1900, the extensive factory known as Stoke Pottery (then owned by Mr. James Plant) was acquired, and also the business of the Winton Pottery Co., Ltd. These three firms were amalgamated, and formed into a Company which was incorporated under the title of "GRIMWADES LIMITED," Mr. L. L. Grimwade being appointed Chairman and Managing Director.

Stoke Pottery being adjacent to the canal, and comprising in addition to a large range of ovens and kilns, a complete equipment for milling the raw materials, including flint, and Cornish stone, enabled the new Company to improve the texture and body of its wares, and also insure only the **best materials** being used in the manufacture of same.

During the same year, the lease was purchased of a fine building in St. Andrew St., London, where the well-known show-rooms of the firm were established, and this building has since become known as " WINTON HOUSE." Here a complete range of goods have been constantly on show, under the genial and skilful superintendence of Mr. John Sayer.

The Directors of the new Company were originally :—

Mr. Leonard L. Grimwade
(Chairman and Managing Director).

Mr. Sidney Grimwade.

Mr. Edward Grimwade.

Mr. James Plant.

Mr. T. Watkin.

Subsequently Mr. Sidney Grimwade and Mr. Edward Grimwade retired from the Board, and Mr. William James and Mr. J. Wilfred Graham were appointed Directors. Mr. James manages the extensive Foreign and Export business of the company, and periodically visits Canada and other important Countries in which the firm operates. Mr. Graham superintends the despatch of goods for London and the United Kingdom generally.

In 1901, the Chairman of the Company, Mr. L. L. Grimwade, inaugurated a series of experiments in improved methods of kiln-firing, and at great cost of time and money, developed enamel firing in what are known as Climax Rotary Kilns, whereby a large saving in fuel is effected and orders can be executed more expeditiously. But more important than the economy effected was the improved results obtained. Brighter and more lustrous colours, with durable and more brilliant gold, gained for the productions of the firm, an added reputation. These improvements in firing were severely tested by the enormous rush of orders which occurred at the time of the Coronation of King Edward VII. in 1902. Nearly half a million Souvenirs were produced by the firm within a very few weeks. Unfortunately just before the date of the Coronation, a disastrous fire occurred at Stoke Pottery (whereby 100 workpeople were thrown out of employment) and a still more disastrous fire occurred at Winton Pottery, 80,000 souvenir pieces, ready for despatch, were destroyed, and only by prodigious efforts were they replaced in time for the eventful day. The Directors resolved while the fire was still raging, that *at any cost*, all Coronation orders should be completed *to time*. By a supreme effort, this was achieved, and "hot from the kilns" on the very morning they were required, the goods were despatched, some by rail, others by road, and *all delivered in time*.

With the growing popularity of the firm's productions, and to compete with the continually increasing demand, it became necessary to provide further accommodation, so in 1906 the extensive manufactory known as the Brownfield's Works, carried on by The Upper Hanley Pottery Co., Ltd., was acquired. This large and well appointed factory is particularly adapted for trade with the United States of America, Canada, and other important foreign markets. Mr. John Hollinshead, the Managing Director joined the Board of Grimwade's, Ltd., where his wide experience and business acumen have proved invaluable. Later in the same year, the business of the Atlas China Co. (formerly David Chapman & Sons) was acquired, and Grimwades Limited were thereby enabled to cater for their many customers who required high-class China Tea Sets at moderate prices especially suited to a cultured taste. The following year, further extensions being necessary on account of the boom in trade, the business of Messrs. Hines Bros., at "Heron Cross Pottery," Fenton, was purchased, and this extensive pottery with extra large ovens and several enamel kilns added considerably to the Company's facilities.

In order to still further develop the business, and perfect an organization capable of producing all classes of ware, in 1908, the Chairman, Mr. L. L. Grimwade introduced and patented a wide range of domestic articles for Kitchen and Pantry, including the world-famous Quick-Cooker, graciously accepted by Her Majesty, the Queen, during the recent visit to the Potteries This full range of ware included the Flyless Milk Bowl with incurved top for preventing flies contaminating milk, the Hygienic Jug. the Bevel-edged Drainer, the Pie Dish with annular channel and air vents, the Oval Household Jar, and the Perfection Pie Funnel, all of which are recognised as being indispensable for every well-appointed home. They have been certified by the British Institute of Hygiene, and are all protected by Royal Letters Patent. This important development coupled with the advantages that the firm derive from the control of so many factories, has brought the name of " Grimwade " to a leading position in the trade. Supported by a loyal and capable staff, the Directors are able to cope with orders of any magnitude, in such a manner as gives general satisfaction to their many friends and patrons. It is the ambition of the firm to maintain their reputation for progress, hence any suggestions are welcomed (from the staff, or from customers), which are helpful in improving the methods of business, or the suitability of their wares to modern requirements. Correspondence on this point is invited.

The firm have recently purchased the Patent rights of the Grimwade Display Stands which immensely facilitate the artistic arrangement of pottery of all kinds. The stands are supplied at a very reasonable price and have been greatly appreciated by the trade generally. They economise space, and ware can be displayed so effectively that assistants are able to increase sales and serve customers far more expeditiously.

Over a thousand workpeople are employed by the firm, and everything possible in the way of well-lighted and thoroughly ventilated workshops are provided to preserve the health of the employees.

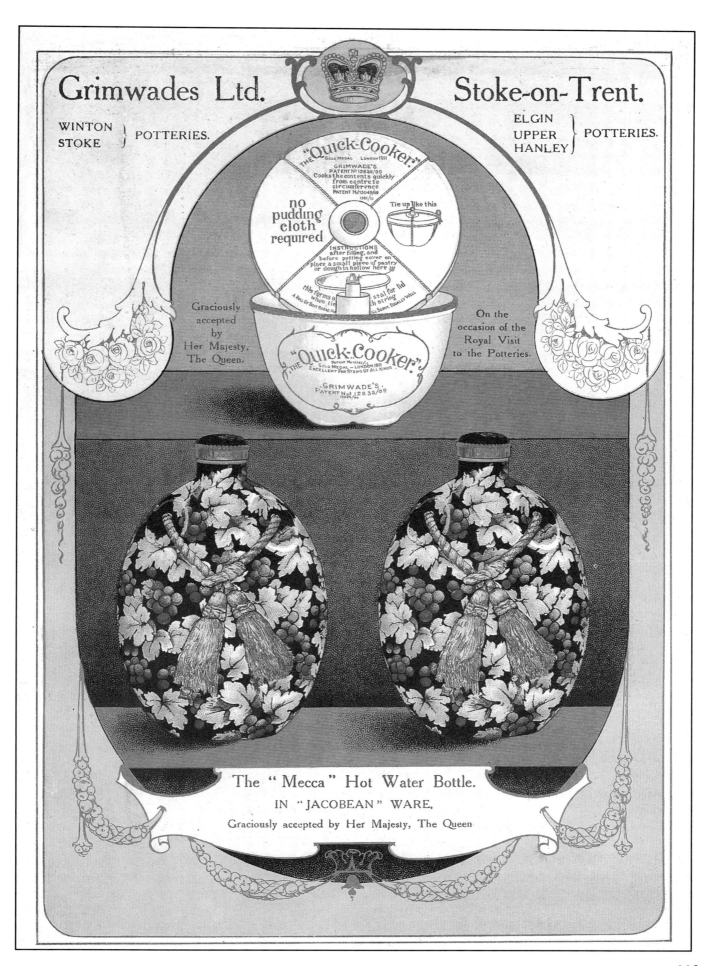

Grimwades Ltd.   Stoke-on-Trent.

WINTON }   ELGIN }
STOKE   } POTTERIES.   UPPER } POTTERIES.
                                                  HANLEY }

"Quick-Cooker"
Gold Medal London 1911
GRIMWADE'S
PATENT No 12835/09
Cooks the contents quickly
from centre to
circumference
PATENT No 15048/09

no
pudding
cloth
required

Tie up like this

INSTRUCTIONS
after filling, and
before putting cover on
place a small piece of pastry
or dough in hollow here

this forms a perfect seal for lid
when tied with string

"Quick-Cooker"
PATENT No 12835/09
Gold Medal — London 1911
EXCELLENT FOR STEWS OF ALL KINDS
GRIMWADE'S
PATENT No 12835/09

Graciously
accepted
by
Her Majesty,
The Queen.

On the
occasion of the
Royal Visit
to the Potteries.

The "Mecca" Hot Water Bottle.

IN "JACOBEAN" WARE,

Graciously accepted by Her Majesty, The Queen.

113

Press Notices.

The Graphic

MESSRS. GRIMWADES EXHIBIT.

"It would be more difficult to describe in these pages the varied products of the Potteries than it was for their Majesties to go over some of the works, though that in itself was a feat which the 'Five Towns' will not readily forget. The Royal party had a chance of seeing a great many products of Staffordshire in the representative exhibition in the King's Hall at Stoke-on-Trent, and some of these we now deal with. Messrs. Grimwade's 'Jacobean' Ware for hall, study, dining-room or boudoir is a delightful production in the style of seventeenth century tapestry. The design is an arrangement of vine leaves, treated conventionally with dark background, which gives charming relief. The warmth of tone is assisted by a rich treatment of the fruitage. A fine range of toilet ware was shown in this decoration, also some lovely jardinières. Two foot-warmers in the ware (on the famous Mecca shape) were presented to her Majesty.

The 'Copenhagen' Ware is produced in the soft greys of the famous faience from which it takes its name. By the introduction of a few warmer tones the requirements of modern furnishings are aptly met.

The 'Royal Hampton' Ware produced by the same firm is very pretty and decorative. One of its merits is that it is produced at such reasonable prices as appeal to the million. The 'Hampton Chintz' Ware, like the above, but with a background of seventeenth century cretonne in old-gold colour finished with green, is particularly suited to toilet ware on the new Weimar shape. The 'Seville' Ware is a conventional treatment of oranges in bold relief on pearly grey-blue ground arranged in the form of a circular panel, with a background in contrasting colours, the embossed outline being thrown into relief by hand work in rich brown.

The firm also showed two ewers and basins in dark blue and gold, one a study of Highland cattle by Austin, the other an old Dutch scene by Bailes, two of the firm's artists.

The Grimwade 'Hygienic Domestic Pottery' for kitchen and pantry use is made of fine white semi-porcelain. The forms have been modelled specially without corners or angles, and can, therefore, easily be cleansed. The most noticeable is the famous 'Quick-Cooker' Bowl, as an ingenious device to ensure the more thorough cooking of food. It is constructed with a central funnel, through which the water boils, thereby cooking thoroughly from centre to sides. It is more wholesome in use, for, having a tight-fitting lid, no cloth is required. It has been certificated by the Institute of Hygiene, and was awarded a gold medal at the Festival of Empire. Another ingenious device is the fly-proof milk-bowl. This has an incurved top to prevent flies getting into milk. It is made in nine sizes, ranging from that required for small families to the largest of all, suitable for use in dairies. A set of both of these was presented to the Queen, who on seeing the cooker exclaimed, ' What a useful thing!' The Grimwade Patent Pie-Dish has an annular channel to prevent burning at bottom, and the 'Perfection' Pie-funnel, oval in form, is fitted to the pie-dish, and so constructed as to ensure light pastry. Another interesting article is the oval Household Jar, with cover for use as a scoop. The collection of dinner ware patterns in all prices, from the pure white to most highly decorated sets, shows how well this firm, with their five factories, cater for the great middle-class trade. There was also a collection of novel shapes in hospital and invalid ware, particularly the 'Meinecke' specialities constructed for the sick-room."

The Daily Telegraph.

" At the conclusion of the inspection, their Majesties came to the glass cases in which the gifts offered and accepted by the King and Queen were displayed. The presents embrace some superb specimens of the potters' art. Amongst them was a patent **Quick Cooker** pudding basin, which requires no pudding cloth. The white stone lid gives diagrams of how it is to be used, with the words : 'Excellent for stews of all kinds. Meat can be kept hot for hours without re-cooking or getting dry.' As the King passed, a member of his suite laughingly drew his attention to the pudding basin. **'What is it?'** his Majesty asked, and on the device being explained the Queen remarked, **' What a useful thing !'** "

The Daily Mail.

"The largest individual display is contributed by MESSRS. GRIMWADES, whose well-known 'Winton Pottery ' is shown in practically every form to meet the requirements of the table or household, whether for use or ornament. Among the various wares, executed in this attractive style of faience, are the Jacobean, decorated in the style of seventeenth century tapestry, with a design formed by an arrangement of vine leaves, treated conventionally with a dark background and carried out in warm rich tones; the 'Royal Hampton,' the patterning of which is taken from the Queen Anne chintz and executed in rich pink, black, and green, the 'Ecla,' which in its lustrous coloration recalls the stained glass of the Renaissance; the 'Seville,' where a conventional treatment of oranges on a pearly grey-blue ground forms the leading decorative motif; and the ' Royal Dorset' limited to flower pots— in which the design consists of massed roses in brilliant tints on a jet black ground. Other exhibits include some highly successful reproductions of the soft grey tones and artistic decoration of the well-known Copenhagen ware; and a number of ingenious appliances for the cooking and preservation of food; and various types of strong and useful dinner ware.

Display of "Grimwade" Ware, at the Potteries Exhibition,
as inspected by their Majesties King George V. and Queen Mary, at the King's Hall, Stoke-on-Trent.

The Potteries' present, which is to be sent on to Buckingham Palace, was also a source of great gratification to her Majesty. Fifty firms have contributed to the gift, which includes every type of pottery and earthenware, from beautiful black basalt and delicate pierced work to a patent cooker, which the Queen declared 'must be very useful.'"

The Daily Dispatch.

GIFTS FOR THE QUEEN.
Her Majesty impressed with Household Utensil.

"At the conclusion of the ceremony the Royal party left the platform for an inspection of the exhibits, and an interesting little incident occurred when they passed one of the four cases containing gifts for the Queen. The King's attention was drawn to a kitchen utensil described as a **Quick Cooker.** He had to ask what its uses were, but the Queen more quickly grasped its possibilities, and remarked, 'I am sure it is a very useful thing.'"

The Standard.

COTTAGE COMFORTS.

Re EXHIBIT AT HARRODS.

"When the royal party reached the large glass case in which the gifts to the Queen were shown, her Majesty had some little incident of interest to tell Princess Mary about every one. She told of the works she had visited, where she saw many of the goods in process of manufacture, and pointed out some of the paintings that she had seen the artists at work on. It was clear that her Majesty was a pottery enthusiast, and her admiration was not only for the designs of magnificent ornamentation, but also for the little housewifely conveniences that make for cottage comfort. Amongst these latter, Grimwade's patent quick-cooking pudding bowl, which is designed to prevent all stodginess in the middle of the pudding, came in for special admiration. It is, therefore, not only her Majesty's interest in the welfare of the industry, but also her keen taste and wide knowledge of the wares produced that has made this exhibition the success it is and given the local potters of North Staffordshire a strong and undoubted claim on the public of Great Britain.

JACOBEAN WARE.

Messrs. Grimwades (Limited), of the Winton Pottery, have discovered quite a new and striking decoration in their Jacobean ware, which has commanded admiration since it was first exhibited. It is a rich arrangement of autumn vine leaves on a black background. Two Mecca-shaped footwarmers in this ware are amongst the Queen's presents. This decoration is also very effectively banded on toilet ware. Jardinières in the new 'Copenhagen' pattern and the quick-cooking bowl with central funnel referred to above are also worthy of careful inspection. It is specially adapted to puddings and stews, and is so arranged that the centre part cooks as soon as the outside. 'A most useful article,' remarked her Majesty when she saw it. It will prove itself a blessing to cooks—professional or amateur."

Directors :

Mr. L. L. Grimwade, *Chairman.*

Mr. James Plant.   Mr. W. James,

Mr. T. Watkin,   Mr. John Hollinshead,

Mr. J. Wilfred Graham.

Representatives :

LONDON :
Mr. JOHN SAYER, and
Mr. BERTRAM J. WOODROFFE.

MIDLAND & SOUTH & WEST OF ENGLAND :
Mr. MARTYN THOMPSON.

NORTH OF ENGLAND, SCOTLAND & IRELAND :
Mr. GEORGE MALKIN.

AUSTRALIA :
Messrs. RESLAW, GREEN & Co.,
163, Pitt Street, SYDNEY.

NEW ZEALAND :
Messrs. H. E. COOPER & Co.,
Hobson Buildings, AUCKLAND.

CANADA :
Mr. G. O. COALES,
122, Wellington Street, West,
TORONTO.

INDIA :
COMMERCIAL EAST INDIA Co.,
83, Old China Bazar Street, CALCUTTA.
THE MALL, LAHORE, and
Messrs. TOTHILL, SHARP & Co.,
BOMBAY.

SOUTH AFRICA :
Mr. T. A. VALLANCE,
JOHANNESBURG & CAPE TOWN.
(P.O. Box 6188)   (P.O. Box 737):

SOUTH AMERICA :
Mr. AIKMAN, Mr. HENDERSON,
and Mr EVANS.

UNITED STATES of AMERICA :
Mr. R. SLIMMON,
96, Church Street, NEW YORK.

SWEDEN :
HERR HERMANN DERLIEN,
30, Smolandsgatan, STOCKHOLM.

NORWAY :
HERR ANDREAS MOE, TRONDHJEM.

HAMBURG :
HERR CARL PFERDMENGES,
Barkhof I,II, HAMBURG.

Yours faithfully

Leonard L Grimwade

Chairman of the Board.

Directors.

T. Watkin.

W. James.

James Plant.

John Hollinshead.

J. Wilfred Graham.

London Showrooms.

TOILET WARE, AND DINNER WARE.

A Corner of
One of the
SAMPLE ROOMS
AT
WINTON HOUSE,
13, St, Andrew St,
LONDON,E.C.

(Grimwades, Ltd.)

One of the Warehouses at Winton Pottery (Grimwades, Ltd.)

The Dinner Ware Showroom, Winton Pottery (Grimwades, Ltd.)

The Toilet Ware Showroom, Winton Pottery (Grimwades, Ltd.)

Mould Makers' Shop, Winton Pottery (Grimwades, Ltd.)

Platemaking at Stoke Pottery (Grimwades, Ltd.)

Aerographing for decorating by compressed air (Grimwades, Ltd.)

Gilding and Enamelling the Royal Winton Ware (Grimwades, Ltd.)

An interesting gathering at the Town Hall, Hanley, to celebrate the Silver Wedding of Mr. & Mrs. L. L. Grimwade in 1911, when a handsome Silver Rose Bowl was presented by the Employees.

"Jacobean" Ware.

No. 3000. "Bute" Flower Pot.
9 in., 8 in., 7 in., 6 in. and 5 in.

No. 3000. "Delphic" Flower Pot.
8 in., 7 in. and 6 in.

No. 2999. "Octagon"

No. 3000. "Octagon" Shape.

No. 3000. "Silver" Shape.

No. 2999. "Wem"

No. 3000. "Wem" Shape.

No. 3000. "Alton" Shape.

"Seville" Ware.

No. 2813.
8 in. and 7 in.

No. 2900.
8 in. and 7 in.

No. 2809.

No. 2813.

No. 2811.

No. 2900.

No. 2812.

No. 2815.

26

"Hampton" Chintz.

No. 562.   "Roma" Shape.

No. 544.   "Etona" Shape.

No. 561.   "Alton" Shape.

No. 544.   "Beaumont" Shape.

No. 564.   "Weimar" Shape.

No. 579.   "Octagon" Shape.

No. 579.   "Riviera" Shape.

No. 561.   "Saxe" Shape.

27

"Copenhagen" Pattern,

No. 570.

"Niobe" Shape.
9 in. and 8 in.

"Delphic" Shape.
8 in., 7 in. and 6 in.

No. 570.   "Wem" Shape.

No. 570.   "Weimar" Shape.

No. 570.   "Bute" Shape.

No. 570.   "Silver" Shape.

No. 570.   "Alton" Shape.

No. 570.   "Saxe" Shape.

28

"Ribbon Chintz" Toilet Ware.

No. C 358.   Ribbon.

No. C 356.   Ribbon.

No. C 355.   Ribbon.

No. C 366.   Ribbon.

No. C 337.   Ribbon.

No. C 335.   Ribbon.

No. C 381.   New Ribbon.

No. C 336.   New Ribbon.

29

"Spode Chintz."

No. 542. "Shan" Shape.

No. 542. "Weimar" Shape.

No. 537. "Weimar"

No. 525. "Etona" Shape.

No. 525. "Kabyle" Shape.

No. 525. "Duval"

No. 542. "Saxe" Shape.

No. 542. "Tara" Shape.

No. 542.
"Mecca" Hot Water Bottle.
30

Solid
Art Toilets.
GUARANTEED
IMPERVIOUS.

"Wem" Shape.
Crushed Strawberry.

"Stuart" Shape.
Crushed Strawberry.

"Stuart" Shape. Russian Green.

"Stuart" Shape. Turquoise.

"Wem" Shape. Dresden Green.

"Wem" Shape. Wedgwood Blue.

"Tientsin" Shape. Yellow.

"Wem" Shape. Heliotrope.

31

PRICES OF WARE ILLUSTRATED IN THE SOUVENIR OF THE ROYAL VISIT.

PAGE 25. "JACOBEAN" WARE.

6 piece Toilet Set, "Octagon,"	No. 2,999	...	...	...	**19/6** set.
" " " "	No. 3,000	...	...	...	**25/-** "
" " " "Silver,"	No. 3,000	...	...	...	**25/-** "
" " " "Wem,"	No. 2,999	...	...	...	**16/6** "
" " " "	No. 3,000	...	...	...	**22/6** "
" " " "Alton,"	No. 3,000	...	...	...	**22/6** "
Flower Pots, "Bute,"	No. 3,000, 9 in., **5/-**; 8 in., **4/-**; 7 in., **3/-**; 6 in., **2/6**; 5 in., **2/-**
" " "Delphic,"	No. 3,000, 8 in., **5/-**; 7 in., **4/-**; 6 in., **3/-**

PAGE 26. "SEVILLE" WARE.

6 piece Toilet Set, all colourings	...	...	...	..	**14/6** set.
Flower Pot, No. 2,813 ...	...	...	... 8 in., **2/9**; 7 in., **2/3** each.
" " No. 2,900 ...	..	...	... 8 in., **2/9**; 7 in., **2/3** "

PAGE 27. "HAMPTON CHINTZ."

6 piece Toilet Set, "Roma,"	No. 562	...	...	...	**12/6** set.
" " " "Etona,"	No. 544	...	...	...	**12/6** "
" " " "Alton,"	No. 561	...	...	...	**12/6** "
" " " "Beaumont,"	No. 544	...	...	...	**10/6** "
" " " "Weimar,"	No. 564	...	...	...	**10/6** "
" " " "Octagon,"	No. 579	...	...	...	**13/6** "
" " " "Riviera,"	No. 579	...	...	...	**10/6** "
" " " "Saxe,"	No. 561	...	..	...	**12/6** "

All these designs can be supplied on each shape at prices quoted.

PAGE 28. "COPENHAGEN WARE."

6 piece Toilet Set, "Wem,"	No. 570	..	...	...	**15/6** set.
" " " "Weimar,"	No. 570	...	...	...	**13/6** "
" " " "Bute,"	No. 570	...	...	...	**15/6** "
" " " "Silver,"	No. 570	..	...	...	**14/6** "
" " " "Alton,"	No. 570	...	...	...	**14/6** "
" " " "Saxe,"	No. 570	...	..	...	**14/6** "
Flower Pot, "Niobe,"	No. 570	... 9 in., **3/6**; 8 in., **3/-** each.
" " "Delphic,"	No. 570, 8 in., **3/-**; 7 in., **2/6**; 6 in., **2/-** "

PRICES OF WARE—(Continued).

PAGE 29. "RIBBON CHINTZ."

6 piece Toilet Set, "Ribbon," all colorings as illustrated	...	**7/6**	set.
" " " "New Ribbon" shape, all colorings	...	**8/-**	"

PAGE 30. "SPODE CHINTZ."

6 piece Toilet Set, "Shan,"	No. 542	...	...	...	**10/6**	set.
" " " "Weimar,"	No. 542	...	...	...	**12/6**	"
" " " "	No. 537	...	...	...	**12/6**	"
" " " "Etona,"	No. 525	...	...	...	**14/6**	"
" " " "Kabyle,"	No. 525	...	...	...	**14/6**	"
" " " "Duval,"	No. 525	...	...	...	**16/6**	"
" " " "Saxe,"	No. 542	...	...	...	**14/6**	"
" " " "Tara,"	No. 542	...	...	...	**13/6**	"

"Mecca" Hot Water Bottle, No. 542, 8 in., **48/-**; 5½ in., **42/-**; 4 in., **36/-**; 2 pints, **30/-** dozen.

All the colorings illustrated can be supplied on any of the shapes at the prices quoted.

PAGE 31. SOLID ART TOILETS.

6 piece Toilet Set, "Wem," Strawberry	...	...	..	**12/6**	set.
" " " "Stuart," " ...	...	...	...	**8/6**	"
" " " " Turquoise	...	...	...	**8/6**	"
" " " " Russian Green	..	...	...	**8/6**	"
" " " "Wem," Dresden Green	...	...	...	**12/6**	"
" " " "Tientsin," Yellow ...	...	...	...	**7/-**	"
" " " "Wem," Wedgwood Blue	...	...	...	**13/6**	"
" " " " Heliotrope	..	...	...	**13/6**	"

All the colorings illustrated can be applied to any shape (Wedgwood Blue and Heliotrope, 1/- extra).

Display Stands, Stained Mahogany Fittings, Silver Plated Metal Work, £5 5s. 0d. nett.

GRIMWADES, Ltd.,

STOKE-ON-TRENT.

INDEX

BIBLIOGRAPHY

"The Chintz Collector Newsletter." Pasadena, California. Various issues.

Eberle, Linda and Susan Scott. *The Charlton Standard Catalogue of Chintz*. 2nd Edition. Birmingham, Michigan: The Charlton Press, 1997.

Edwards, Anne. *Royal Sisters: Queen Elizabeth II and Princess Margaret*. New York: William Morrow and Company, 1990.

The Glass and China Trader. England. April 1913, May 1913, August 1913, November 1913, August 1916.

Godden, Geoffrey A. *Encyclopedia of British Pottery and Porcelain Marks*. London, England: Herbert Jenkins Ltd., 1964.

Hawley, T. "Sketches of Pottery Life and Character." Staffordshire, England: 1906.

Hughes, Bernard and Therle. *The Collector's Encyclopaedia of English Ceramics*. London, England: Abbey Library, 1967.

McCoy, Elin. "Tea, It's Just the Cure." *Reader's Digest Magazine*. June 1997.

Miller, Muriel. *Collecting Royal Winton Chintz*. London, England: Francis Joseph, 1996.

---. *The Royal Winton Collectors Handbook From 1925*. London, England: Francis Joseph, 1998.

Price Guide to Majolica. Gas City, Indiana: L-W Book Sales and Publishing, 1997.

"The Royal Winton International Collector's Club Newsletter." Dancer's End, Northall, England. Various issues.

GUIDE TO ROYAL WINTON VALUES

Prices listed in the next section reflect asking prices and not necessarily the actual selling price. Values differ according to geographical region, popularity of the pattern, or condition of the item. Availability and demand are other important considerations, as are markings, because they can indicate the age of a piece.

Anything with easily broken parts—handles, lids, etc.—can bring a higher price because fewer survive intact (for example, breakfast or bedside sets, with many small pieces). Teapots are another scarce item, since they were so frequently used.

VALUES

The sudden popularity of Royal Winton chintz has resulted in phenomenal price increases. Identical pieces with other decorations, such as lustre, souvenir or pastel ware, may be priced lower. This is changing, however, as new collectors discover the beauty and charm of other non-chintz pieces like Rosebud and Cottage ware, steadily gaining in popularity and value.

Fashion and price are linked, but it can be misleading to declare one pattern or another more expensive based solely on its popularity. Taste and popularity vary from one region to another, and change over time.

Antique shop prices reflect what the dealer feels is the correct market value of the piece, plus how much he or she paid for the piece. Book prices can only be a guide, reflecting an average of those asked; when calculating an average price, the majority rules. I have seen shop prices that vary according to hundreds—even thousands—of dollars (or pounds) from any published book price. For example, a Julia bedside set may sell for $4500, whereas its listed book price is $1600.

Auction prices can be misleading and do not always reflect true market value. If buyers get carried away in a bidding frenzy, they might end up paying much more than market value. Or, they may buy an unopened box for very little and find a treasure trove. If you buy at an auction, keep in mind that there will be selling charges added to the price, and a 15% VAT (value added tax) in England.

CONDITION

Finding every piece in pristine or perfect condition is the ideal, perhaps unrealistic goal. Some pieces have consistently weathered the years better than others, but time does take its toll. Pattern or glaze can rub off, color becomes less vivid, and lustre might dim with age and wear. Chips, cracks and repairs usually do—and should affect price. However, a hard-to-find piece with a repair, hairline crack or chip may be priced at only a few dollars less than a perfect piece.

Some dealers consider a chip under an item to be a "no-fault" flaw that doesn't detract from the price, and charge full value. Buyers with an eye for completing a perfect collection may be unwilling to pay full value for a damaged piece. Realistically, a 70-year old piece of china or pottery will show some crazing and wear, which actually helps to authenticate its age.

There are professionals who, for a price, repair and restore pottery and china. The service is not cheap, nor will it make a damaged piece new again. But, if well done, it may bring the piece back or close to full value. A well preserved or carefully restored item is a piece of the past and a tribute to years of loving care.

QUALITY

Remember, what you see is what you get. The rule is *caveat emptor* (buyer beware). Before buying, inspect the piece carefully. Run your hand along the edges, to find small chips. Hold it up to the light, checking for cracks or mends. Better yet, take along a magnifying glass. It is worth taking this extra time; once you purchase an item, it is very difficult to get a refund on the premise that you didn't notice a flaw or damage. Reputable dealers will mark a damaged piece "as is" or "as found," if they know it has been damaged or repaired. Still, it is possible for them to miss something, too.

WHAT TO COLLECT

Building a collection is time-consuming, but that's part of the fun. It will take time to collect a toast rack in every chintz pattern, for example. But collecting one in every Rosebud design might be easier. Toast racks are more easily found in England, since British households prefer their toast crisp and unbuttered, unlike Americans who serve it buttered on a plate.

The colors in pastel, lustre, Rosebud and chintz ware blend together beautifully, opening up possibilities for collectors to mix and match items. This allows for a unique look at a lesser expense. For example, a pastel saucer can be paired with a chintz cup, or used as an underliner. A Rosebud candlestick, serving bowl or teapot will blend beautifully with most chintz.

Trading with other collectors is a good way to build a collection. But remember that it is your collection, and you make the rules. If it pleases you, go for it. Whatever your goal, completing a collection is not always the end of the search, but may lead to the start of another. In the final analysis, a piece is only worth what someone is willing to pay. Richard and I explored antique malls, shows and shops across the country, and in England and Canada. Prices listed in this book, unless otherwise noted, reflect the retail value for items or sets in undamaged or well-restored condition. We calculated an average based on values found in antique shops, shows, and on the Internet. Any price that varies wildly from the norm (for example, a chintz teapot that sold for $4200), has not been considered in averaging.

1998 PRICE GUIDE

Prices are listed for the United States and England, however money exchange rates can change daily. I did not take the U. S. price and calculate the British price according to the exchange rate. Instead, I went by the prices I actually found in various parts of England on my numerous trips there, including the Newark Show where thousands of dealers were present. Some pieces are more, or less, expensive in one country than the other

Finally, neither the publisher nor the author can accept responsibility or liability for losses incurred by persons using this guide as the basis for any transaction, whether due to typographical errors or other reasons.

FIGURE		U. S. $	U. K. £	FIGURE		U. S. $	U. K. £	FIGURE		U. S. $	U. K. £
1	–	135.00	65.00	14	–	150.00	85.00	26	–	45.00	25.00
2	–	225.00	110.00	15	–	135.00	70.00	27	–	250.00	95.00
3	–	135.00	60.00	16	–	110.00	65.00	28	–	85.00	60.00
4	–	135.00	85.00	17	–	125.00	60.00	29	–	85.00	60.00
5	–	135.00	85.00	18	–	70.00	25.00	30	–	165.00	65.00
6	–	85.00	30.00	19	–	110.00	70.00	31	–	45.00	25.00
7	–	100.00	65.00	19A	–	45.00	20.00	32	–	150.00	80.00
8	–	225.00	100.00	20	–	125.00	75.00	33	–	165.00	75.00
9	–	125.00	60.00	21	–	575.00	350.00	34	–	75.00	35.00
10	–	210.00	120.00	22	–	110.00	60.00	35	–	55.00	20.00
11	–	35.00	15.00	23	–	45.00	20.00	36	–	60.00	40.00
12	–	65.00	35.00	24	–	375.00	125.00	37	–	50.00	25.00
13	–	75.00	45.00	25	–	165.00	75.00	38	–	60.00	35.00

Figure		U. S. $	U. K. £	Figure		U. S. $	U. K. £	Figure		U. S. $	U. K. £
39	–	525.00	275.00	80	–	110.00	35.00	122	–	160.00	65.00
40	–	65.00	30.00	81	–	55.00	25.00	123	–	150.00	75.00
41	–	1250.00	600.00	82	–	175.00	95.00	124	–	90.00	40.00
42	–	325.00	200.00	83	–	175.00	95.00	125	–	90.00	40.00
43	–	750.00	400.00	84	–	295.00	150.00	126	–	120.00	45.00
44	–	75.00	30.00	85	–	295.00	150.00	127	–	60.00	30.00
45	–	135.00	75.00	86	–	295.00	150.00	128	–	95.00	35.00
45A	–	175.00	110.00	87	–	395.00	250.00	129	–	65.00	30.00
46	–	65.00	35.00	88	–	110.00	50.00	130	–	60.00	30.00
47	–	50.00	20.00	89	–	110.00	50.00	131	–	65.00	35.00
48	–	155.00	55.00	90	–	125.00	50.00	132	–	50.00	25.00
49	–	50.00	25.00	91	–	295.00	85.00	133	–	65.00	35.00
50	–	125.00	55.00	92	–	175.00	95.00	134	–	55.00	25.00
51	–	85.00	40.00	93	–	225.00	90.00	135	–	65.00	30.00
52	–	50.00	20.00	94	–	225.00	90.00	136	–	165.00	45.00
53	–	50.00	20.00	95	–	350.00	100.00	137	–	250.00	75.00
54	–	75.00	25.00	96	–	210.00	85.00	138	–	50.00	20.00
55	–	135.00	45.00	97	–	350.00	90.00	139	–	20.00	5.00
56	–	75.00	30.00	98	–	175.00	70.00	140	–	45.00	15.00
57	–	55.00	25.00	99	–	125.00	40.00	141	–	65.00	25.00
58	–	75.00	35.00	100	–	125.00	35.00	142	–	30.00	10.00
59	–	200.00	95.00	101	–	150.00	50.00	143	–	250.00	75.00
60	–	145.00	75.00	102	–	195.00	45.00	144	–	45.00	20.00
61	–	185.00	75.00	103	–	85.00	35.00	145	–	165.00	50.00
62	–	65.00	25.00	104	–	85.00	35.00	146	–	95.00	35.00
63	–	65.00	25.00	105	–	110.00	50.00	147	–	95.00	35.00
64	–	135.00	60.00	106	–	145.00	45.00	148	–	165.00	40.00
65	–	65.00	25.00	107	–	450.00	225.00	149	–	165.00	40.00
66	–	85.00	30.00	108	–	135.00	50.00	150	–	65.00	30.00
67	–	65.00	25.00	109	–	175.00	55.00	151	–	45.00	15.00
68	–	75.00	30.00	110	–	225.00	70.00	152	–	65.00	30.00
69	–	125.00	65.00	111	–	150.00	70.00	153	–	50.00	20.00
70	–	75.00	35.00	112	–	350.00	100.00	154	–	40.00	15.00
71	–	65.00	25.00	113	–	225.00	80.00	155	–	50.00	20.00
72	–	85.00	30.00	114	–	150.00	70.00	156	–	40.00	15.00
73	–	65.00	25.00	115	–	150.00	85.00	157	–	75.00	25.00
74	–	175.00	85.00	116	–	75.00	25.00	158	–	65.00	25.00
75	–	65.00	30.00	117	–	125.00	65.00	159	–	55.00	20.00
76	–	125.00	60.00	118	–	125.00	50.00	160	–	75.00	25.00
77	–	150.00	85.00	119	–	195.00	70.00	161	–	75.00	25.00
78	–	100.00	35.00	120	–	215.00	85.00	162	–	65.00	25.00
79	–	55.00	25.00	121	–	195.00	125.00	163	–	40.00	15.00

Figure		U. S. $	U. K. £	Figure		U. S. $	U. K. £	Figure		U. S. $	U. K. £
164	–	40.00	15.00	206	–	125.00	50.00	248	–	375.00	110.00
165	–	75.00	30.00	207	–	105.00	35.00	249	–	275.00	135.00
166	–	75.00	25.00	208	–	95.00	45.00	250	–	200.00	90.00
167	–	95.00	35.00	209	–	85.00	40.00	251	–	200.00	95.00
168	–	110.00	40.00	210	–	95.00	35.00	252	–	195.00	90.00
169	–	195.00	95.00	211	–	75.00	25.00	253	–	245.00	100.00
170	–	135.00	45.00	212	–	195.00	70.00	254	–	195.00	90.00
171	–	135.00	50.00	213	–	95.00	35.00	255	–	210.00	90.00
172	–	135.00	50.00	214	–	215.00	95.00	256	–	235.00	110.00
173	–	110.00	45.00	215	–	75.00	25.00	257	–	195.00	90.00
174	–	85.00	35.00	216	–	65.00	30.00	258	–	135.00	55.00
175	–	450.00	110.00	217	–	110.00	45.00	259	–	135.00	55.00
176	–	115.00	55.00	218	–	145.00	70.00	260	–	95.00	50.00
177	–	135.00	75.00	219	–	85.00	35.00	261	–	135.00	55.00
178	–	135.00	55.00	220	–	195.00	55.00	262	–	35.00	15.00
179	–	100.00	50.00	221	–	165.00	60.00	263	–	30.00	10.00
180	–	175.00	75.00	222	–	85.00	35.00	264	–	65.00	25.00
181	–	225.00	90.00	223	–	85.00	35.00	265	–	95.00	35.00
182	–	225.00	90.00	224	–	125.00	45.00	266	–	40.00	15.00
183	–	125.00	65.00	225	–	65.00	20.00	267	–	35.00	15.00
184	–	235.00	85.00	226	–	85.00	35.00	268	–	85.00	30.00
185	–	115.00	60.00	227	–	110.00	40.00	269	–	75.00	30.00
186	–	145.00	60.00	228	–	110.00	40.00	270	–	40.00	20.00
187	–	210.00	95.00	229	–	110.00	45.00	271	–	75.00	30.00
188	–	275.00	110.00	230	–	60.00	30.00	272	–	95.00	35.00
189	–	175.00	80.00	231	–	65.00	30.00	273	–	35.00	15.00
190	–	75.00	30.00	232	–	65.00	30.00	274	–	30.00	10.00
191	–	110.00	45.00	233	–	60.00	30.00	275	–	35.00	15.00
192	–	250.00	95.00	234	–	110.00	45.00	276	–	75.00	30.00
193	–	100.00	55.00	235	–	70.00	30.00	277	–	125.00	40.00
194	–	95.00	45.00	236	–	475.00	125.00	278	–	85.00	35.00
195	–	90.00	45.00	237	–	125.00	45.00	279	–	85.00	35.00
196	–	90.00	45.00	238	–	275.00	85.00	280	–	85.00	40.00
197	–	125.00	50.00	239	–	60.00	20.00	281	–	70.00	25.00
198	–	125.00	50.00	240	–	185.00	60.00	282	–	175.00	65.00
199	–	100.00	50.00	241	–	110.00	55.00	283	–	165.00	65.00
200	–	100.00	45.00	242	–	425.00	110.00	284	–	125.00	50.00
201	–	125.00	50.00	243	–	105.00	50.00	285	–	75.00	30.00
202	–	125.00	50.00	244	–	475.00	200.00	286	–	65.00	25.00
203	–	125.00	50.00	245	–	325.00	125.00	287	–	75.00	25.00
204	–	85.00	45.00	246	–	225.00	100.00	288	–	95.00	25.00
205	–	115.00	50.00	247	–	245.00	95.00	289	–	45.00	20.00

Figure		U. S. $	U. K. £	Figure		U. S. $	U. K. £	Figure		U. S. $	U. K. £
290	–	55.00	25.00	332	–	85.00	40.00	374	–	50.00	30.00
291	–	45.00	15.00	333	–	65.00	25.00	375	–	95.00	35.00
292	–	55.00	25.00	334	–	135.00	35.00	376	–	55.00	25.00
293	–	60.00	20.00	335	–	125.00	50.00	377	–	55.00	25.00
294	–	135.00	65.00	336	–	195.00	55.00	378	–	75.00	35.00
295	–	65.00	25.00	337	–	350.00	135.00	379	–	45.00	25.00
296	–	55.00	25.00	338	–	85.00	40.00	380	–	35.00	20.00
297	–	95.00	30.00	339	–	115.00	45.00	381	–	75.00	35.00
298	–	95.00	30.00	340	–	225.00	85.00	382	–	40.00	25.00
299	–	85.00	25.00	341	–	85.00	35.00	383	–	55.00	25.00
300	–	125.00	50.00	342	–	150.00	60.00	384	–	65.00	35.00
301	–	145.00	75.00	343	–	140.00	55.00	385	–	35.00	20.00
302	–	125.00	60.00	344	–	125.00	50.00	386	–	40.00	25.00
303	–	65.00	20.00	345	–	125.00	40.00	387	–	40.00	25.00
304	–	425.00	125.00	346	–	125.00	40.00	388	–	40.00	25.00
305	–	85.00	30.00	347	–	185.00	65.00	389	–	40.00	25.00
306	–	125.00	55.00	348	–	80.00	35.00	390	–	45.00	25.00
307	–	135.00	40.00	349	–	80.00	35.00	391	–	75.00	35.00
308	–	145.00	65.00	350	–	35.00	15.00	392	–	75.00	35.00
309	–	175.00	65.00	351	–	80.00	40.00	393	–	75.00	35.00
310	–	175.00	70.00	352	–	55.00	25.00	394	–	75.00	35.00
311	–	115.00	45.00	353	–	55.00	25.00	395	–	75.00	35.00
312	–	125.00	60.00	354	–	225.00	75.00	396	–	35.00	20.00
313	–	135.00	45.00	355	–	45.00	20.00	397	–	35.00	20.00
314	–	145.00	80.00	356	–	95.00	30.00	398	–	75.00	40.00
315	–	135.00	45.00	357	–	65.00	25.00	399	–	65.00	30.00
316	–	160.00	75.00	358	–	60.00	25.00	400	–	55.00	25.00
317	–	145.00	50.00	359	–	45.00	15.00	401	–	55.00	25.00
318	–	175.00	70.00	360	–	40.00	15.00	402	–	55.00	25.00
319	–	125.00	65.00	361	–	85.00	30.00	403	–	55.00	25.00
320	–	95.00	45.00	362	–	50.00	25.00	404	–	95.00	40.00
321	–	85.00	40.00	363	–	75.00	30.00	405	–	55.00	25.00
322	–	165.00	65.00	364	–	85.00	35.00	406	–	35.00	20.00
323	–	85.00	35.00	365	–	85.00	30.00	407	–	35.00	15.00
324	–	145.00	50.00	366	–	90.00	30.00	408	–	55.00	25.00
325	–	110.00	40.00	367	–	65.00	25.00	409	–	50.00	25.00
326	–	120.00	30.00	368	–	35.00	20.00	410	–	50.00	25.00
327	–	85.00	30.00	369	–	45.00	20.00	411	–	85.00	45.00
328	–	95.00	40.00	370	–	55.00	25.00	412	–	35.00	20.00
329	–	165.00	65.00	371	–	55.00	25.00	413	–	110.00	55.00
330	–	95.00	35.00	372	–	65.00	30.00	414	–	50.00	25.00
331	–	135.00	40.00	373	–	35.00	10.00	415	–	35.00	20.00

Figure		U. S. $	U. K. £	Figure		U. S. $	U. K. £	Figure		U. S. $	U. K. £
416	–	50.00	25.00	452	–	65.00	30.00	488	–	95.00	25.00
417	–	35.00	20.00	453	–	95.00	40.00	489	–	125.00	40.00
418	–	45.00	25.00	454	–	125.00	55.00	490	–	75.00	30.00
419	–	60.00	30.00	455	–	110.00	50.00	491	–	35.00	20.00
420	–	50.00	25.00	456	–	185.00	60.00	492	–	85.00	35.00
421	–	55.00	25.00	457	–	185.00	60.00	493	–	70.00	25.00
422	–	110.00	40.00	458	–	225.00	65.00	494	–	35.00	15.00
423	–	125.00	50.00	459	–	125.00	50.00	495	–	95.00	30.00
424	–	125.00	55.00	460	–	75.00	35.00	496	–	35.00	15.00
425	–	45.00	15.00	461	–	45.00	15.00	497	–	75.00	25.00
426	–	115.00	40.00	462	–	85.00	30.00	498	–	95.00	35.00
427	–	65.00	30.00	463	–	55.00	25.00	499	–	75.00	30.00
428	–	85.00	45.00	464	–	65.00	25.00	500	–	75.00	30.00
429	–	45.00	15.00	465	–	175.00	65.00	501	–	65.00	25.00
430	–	45.00	15.00	466	–	110.00	35.00	502	–	65.00	25.00
431	–	45.00	15.00	467	–	75.00	30.00	503	–	45.00	20.00
432	–	45.00	15.00	468	–	150.00	65.00	504	–	35.00	15.00
433	–	45.00	15.00	469	–	50.00	25.00	505	–	45.00	20.00
434	–	45.00	15.00	470	–	50.00	25.00	506	–	120.00	35.00
435	–	85.00	35.00	471	–	55.00	30.00	507	–	35.00	15.00
436	–	85.00	35.00	472	–	55.00	30.00	508	–	35.00	15.00
437	–	95.00	40.00	473	–	45.00	20.00	509	–	35.00	15.00
438	–	95.00	40.00	474	–	65.00	25.00	510	–	65.00	30.00
439	–	50.00	20.00	475	–	95.00	35.00	511	–	20.00	10.00
440	–	75.00	35.00	476	–	65.00	25.00	512	–	95.00	45.00
441	–	85.00	40.00	477	–	45.00	15.00	513	–	25.00	15.00
442	–	85.00	40.00	478	–	45.00	15.00	514	–	30.00	15.00
443	–	85.00	40.00	479	–	35.00	10.00	515	–	25.00	15.00
444	–	65.00	30.00	480	–	25.00	10.00	516	–	55.00	30.00
445	–	85.00	40.00	481	–	95.00	35.00	517	–	40.00	20.00
446	–	95.00	40.00	482	–	65.00	30.00	518	–	85.00	40.00
447	–	50.00	20.00	483	–	30.00	15.00	519	–	30.00	10.00
448	–	60.00	25.00	484	–	30.00	15.00	520	–	95.00	45.00
449	–	60.00	25.00	485	–	80.00	40.00	521	–	25.00	15.00
450	–	75.00	35.00	486	–	25.00	10.00				
451	–	60.00	25.00	487	–	35.00	15.00				

COMPREHENSIVE PRICE GUIDE FOR COTTAGE AND ROSEBUD
(ALL ITEMS ARE NOT SHOWN IN BOOK)

COTTAGE WARE

Included in this category are Ye Olde Inne, Ye Olde Mill, Beehive, Olde England, Chanticleer, Lakeland and Pixie. Prices listed are averages, and may vary in some regions depending on popularity and availablility of a pattern.

	U. S. $	U. K. £
Biscuit Barrels	325.00	140.00
Butter, Covered	175.00	85.00
Cheese, Covered	350.00	165.00
Condiment Set (4-pc.)	175.00	70.00
Cream/Milk Jug	150.00	75.00
Hot Water Jug	175.00	85.00
Plates	175.00	75.00
Relish, 3-part Divided	195.00	85.00
Salt/Pepper on Tray	150.00	75.00
Sugar Shakers	210.00	160.00
Teapot	475.00	175.00

ROSEBUD WARE

This category includes Rosebud, Tiger Lily (Honey Lily), Petunia, Fuchsia and Hibiscus. Prices may vary depending on current popularity of design, color, and availability.

	U. S. $	U. K. £
Bedside Sets	1200.00	450.00
Bonbon Dish	135.00	50.00
Bowl, Salad	145.00	75.00
Butter, Covered	225.00	75.00
Cake Plate, Tiered	225.00	85.00
Candlesticks (each)	135.00	35.00
Cheese, Covered	245.00	110.00
Coffee Pot	375.00	150.00
Compote	160.00	75.00
Condiment Set (4-pc.)	175.00	70.00
Cream/Milk Jug	125.00	50.00
Creamer and Sugar	195.00	75.00
Creamer/Sugar on Tray	175.00	65.00
Hot Water Jug	275.00	115.00
Jam Pot	140.00	55.00
Mint Boat w/Underliner	125.00	65.00
Plate, 6" or 7"	85.00	35.00
Plate, 8"	75.00	25.00
Salt/Pepper on Tray	135.00	40.00
Sugar Bowl	75.00	30.00
Teacups and Saucers	115.00	40.00
Teapot	450.00	200.00
Tea Sets for 6 w/Teapot	1250.00	650.00
Tennis Set	125.00	50.00
Toast Rack, 2-slice	145.00	65.00
Toast Rack, 4-slice	165.00	65.00
Trinket Pot	115.00	45.00
Wall Pocket	325.00	125.00

COMPREHENSIVE PRICE GUIDE FOR CHINTZ

	ANEMONE		BALMORAL		BEDALE	
	U. S. $	U. K. £	U. S. $	U. K. £	U. S. $	U. K. £
Bedside, Breakfast Set	600.00	325.00	1200.00	500.00	1000.00	600.00
Bonbon	45.00	30.00	85.00	55.00	88.00	55.00
Bowl, 5"	95.00	45.00	85.00	40.00	75.00	40.00
Butter, Covered	130.00	75.00	195.00	135.00	225.00	125.00
Cake Plate, Open hdl.	125.00	70.00	165.00	130.00	175.00	120.00
Cake Plate, Pedestal	130.00	70.00	170.00	130.00	175.00	125.00
Cake Plate, Tiered	130.00	90.00	180.00	140.00	150.00	120.00
Candy/Sweets Dish	45.00	25.00	75.00	35.00	85.00	40.00
Cheese Keeper, Covd.	450.00	275.00	235.00	170.00	185.00	140.00
Coffee Pot	450.00	310.00	850.00	375.00	550.00	350.00
Compote	140.00	85.00	159.00	120.00	120.00	75.00
Condiment Set on Tray	140.00	85.00	225.00	140.00	165.00	110.00
Creamer and Sugar	95.00	50.00	165.00	95.00	125.00	70.00
Creamer/Sugar on Tray	145.00	80.00	225.00	170.00	175.00	140.00
Demitasse Cup/Saucer	65.00	25.00	95.00	50.00	75.00	45.00
Egg Cup, Footed	45.00	25.00	85.00	60.00	85.00	50.00
Hot Water Jug	200.00	120.00	225.00	125.00	425.00	225.00
Jam Pot w/Underliner	85.00	55.00	175.00	110.00	125.00	105.00
Milk Jug	175.00	120.00	425.00	200.00	375.00	200.00
Pin Tray	45.00	25.00	75.00	35.00	60.00	35.00
Plate, 6"	45.00	25.00	85.00	40.00	55.00	45.00
Plate, 9"	75.00	40.00	135.00	95.00	110.00	65.00
Plate, 10"	89.00	35.00	155.00	100.00	110.00	65.00
Relish	100.00	60.00	175.00	110.00	125.00	80.00
Salad Bowl (Chrome Rim)	110.00	60.00	150.00	115.00	125.00	85.00
Salt/Pepper on Tray	125.00	75.00	185.00	120.00	135.00	90.00
Sauce Boat, Underliner	100.00	65.00	150.00	115.00	125.00	90.00
Teacup and Saucer	70.00	40.00	125.00	60.00	110.00	55.00
Teapot, 2-cup	225.00	165.00	425.00	175.00	300.00	225.00
Teapot, 4-cup	300.00	180.00	650.00	325.00	460.00	375.00
Teapot, 6-cup	450.00	235.00	850.00	475.00	850.00	450.00
Teapot, Stacking	625.00	300.00	950.00	500.00	1000.00	550.00
Tennis Set	75.00	45.00	125.00	75.00	110.00	65.00
Toast Rack, 2-slice	125.00	85.00	165.00	120.00	155.00	115.00
Toast Rack, 4-slice	160.00	110.00	200.00	165.00	225.00	160.00
Trivet	75.00	50.00	100.00	75.00	95.00	65.00
Vase, Bud	85.00	50.00	150.00	105.00	150.00	125.00

COMPREHENSIVE PRICE GUIDE FOR CHINTZ

	BEESTON		BIRDS AND TULIPS		BLUE JADE	
	U. S. $	U. K. £	U. S. $	U. K. £	U. S. $	U. K. £
Bedside, Breakfast Set	1250.00	700.00	750.00	360.00	750.00	360.00
Bonbon	95.00	55.00	75.00	45.00	75.00	45.00
Bowl, 5"	75.00	40.00	65.00	35.00	65.00	35.00
Butter, Covered	275.00	135.00	225.00	85.00	175.00	85.00
Cake Plate, Open hdl.	225.00	160.00	135.00	85.00	135.00	85.00
Cake Plate, Pedestal	245.00	165.00	140.00	95.00	140.00	95.00
Cake Plate, Tiered	250.00	160.00	150.00	100.00	150.00	100.00
Candy/Sweets Dish	85.00	40.00	65.00	35.00	65.00	35.00
Cheese Keeper, Covd.	325.00	210.00	175.00	115.00	175.00	115.00
Coffee Pot	1150.00	600.00	350.00	200.00	350.00	200.00
Compote	220.00	125.00	110.00	65.00	110.00	65.00
Condiment Set on Tray	275.00	150.00	150.00	100.00	150.00	100.00
Creamer and Sugar	125.00	70.00	100.00	60.00	100.00	60.00
Creamer/Sugar on Tray	325.00	200.00	150.00	100.00	150.00	100.00
Demitasse Cup/Saucer	120.00	85.00	75.00	45.00	75.00	45.00
Egg Cup, Footed	105.00	60.00	65.00	30.00	65.00	30.00
Hot Water Jug	575.00	300.00	275.00	150.00	275.00	150.00
Jam Pot w/Underliner	210.00	135.00	125.00	75.00	125.00	75.00
Milk Jug	525.00	300.00	250.00	125.00	250.00	125.00
Pin Tray	95.00	45.00	45.00	25.00	45.00	25.00
Plate, 6"	75.00	40.00	50.00	30.00	50.00	30.00
Plate, 9"	150.00	100.00	60.00	40.00	60.00	40.00
Plate, 10"	175.00	110.00	85.00	60.00	85.00	60.00
Relish	220.00	150.00	125.00	75.00	125.00	75.00
Salad Bowl (Chrome Rim)	195.00	95.00	105.00	60.00	105.00	60.00
Salt/Pepper on Tray	195.00	115.00	150.00	85.00	150.00	85.00
Sauce Boat, Underliner	165.00	115.00	115.00	70.00	115.00	70.00
Teacup and Saucer	135.00	75.00	95.00	45.00	80.00	45.00
Teapot, 2-cup	525.00	300.00	225.00	125.00	225.00	125.00
Teapot, 4-cup	750.00	475.00	350.00	200.00	350.00	200.00
Teapot, 6-cup	1000.00	600.00	475.00	300.00	475.00	300.00
Teapot, Stacking	1200.00	650.00	650.00	425.00	650.00	425.00
Tennis Set	135.00	100.00	85.00	50.00	85.00	50.00
Toast Rack, 2-slice	225.00	135.00	125.00	70.00	125.00	70.00
Toast Rack, 4-slice	325.00	190.00	185.00	120.00	185.00	120.00
Trivet	150.00	85.00	75.00	50.00	75.00	50.00
Vase, Bud	175.00	85.00	100.00	60.00	100.00	60.00

COMPREHENSIVE PRICE GUIDE FOR CHINTZ

	BLUE TULIP		CARNATION		CHEADLE	
	U. S. $	U. K. £	U. S. $	U. K. £	U. S. $	U. K. £
Bedside, Breakfast Set	650.00	325.00			1100.00	325.00
Bonbon	45.00	30.00			45.00	30.00
Bowl, 5"	95.00	45.00			95.00	45.00
Butter, Covered	130.00	75.00			175.00	75.00
Cake Plate, Open hdl.	125.00	70.00			125.00	70.00
Cake Plate, Pedestal	130.00	70.00			130.00	70.00
Cake Plate, Tiered	130.00	90.00			130.00	90.00
Candy/Sweets Dish	45.00	25.00			45.00	25.00
Cheese Keeper, Covd.	450.00	275.00			325.00	175.00
Coffee Pot	450.00	310.00			850.00	500.00
Compote	140.00	85.00			140.00	85.00
Condiment Set on Tray	140.00	85.00			145.00	85.00
Creamer and Sugar	95.00	50.00	175.00	95.00	110.00	70.00
Creamer/Sugar on Tray	145.00	80.00			150.00	145.00
Demitasse Cup/Saucer	65.00	25.00			75.00	45.00
Egg Cup, Footed	45.00	25.00			85.00	50.00
Hot Water Jug	200.00	120.00			425.00	225.00
Jam Pot w/Underliner	85.00	55.00			125.00	95.00
Milk Jug	175.00	120.00			375.00	200.00
Pin Tray	45.00	25.00			55.00	35.00
Plate, 6"	45.00	25.00			55.00	35.00
Plate, 9"	75.00	40.00	8" 145.00	105.00	125.00	65.00
Plate, 10"	89.00	35.00	11" 215.00	115.00	150.00	115.00
Relish	100.00	60.00			150.00	110.00
Salad Bowl (Chrome Rim)	110.00	60.00	175.00	90.00	135.00	95.00
Salt/Pepper on Tray	125.00	75.00			150.00	110.00
Sauce Boat, Underliner	100.00	65.00			135.00	85.00
Teacup and Saucer	70.00	40.00	125.00	70.00	110.00	65.00
Teapot, 2-cup	225.00	165.00	450.00	125.00	225.00	165.00
Teapot, 4-cup	300.00	180.00			300.00	160.00
Teapot, 6-cup	450.00	235.00			650.00	235.00
Teapot, Stacking	625.00	300.00			950.00	550.00
Tennis Set	75.00	45.00			125.00	100.00
Toast Rack, 2-slice	125.00	85.00			155.00	110.00
Toast Rack, 4-slice	160.00	110.00			235.00	125.00
Trivet	75.00	50.00			95.00	50.00
Vase, Bud	85.00	50.00			225.00	95.00

COMPREHENSIVE PRICE GUIDE FOR CHINTZ

	CHELSEA		CHINTZ		CLEVEDON	
	U. S. $	U. K. £	U. S. $	U. K. £	U. S. $	U. K. £
Bedside, Breakfast Set	1300.00	700.00	600.00	325.00	1250.00	600.00
Bonbon	135.00	70.00	45.00	30.00	125.00	60.00
Bowl, 5"	85.00	40.00	95.00	45.00	65.00	40.00
Butter, Covered	225.00	120.00	130.00	75.00	235.00	135.00
Cake Plate, Open hdl.	190.00	130.00	125.00	70.00	225.00	150.00
Cake Plate, Pedestal	225.00	130.00	130.00	70.00	225.00	150.00
Cake Plate, Tiered	265.00	140.00	130.00	90.00	235.00	150.00
Candy/Sweets Dish	75.00	35.00	45.00	25.00	75.00	45.00
Cheese Keeper, Covd.	265.00	135.00	450.00	275.00	300.00	215.00
Coffee Pot	950.00	650.00	450.00	310.00	850.00	450.00
Compote	210.00	125.00	140.00	85.00	175.00	120.00
Condiment Set on Tray	225.00	135.00	140.00	85.00	265.00	140.00
Creamer and Sugar	130.00	95.00	95.00	50.00	155.00	95.00
Creamer/Sugar on Tray	250.00	150.00	145.00	80.00	275.00	170.00
Demitasse Cup/Saucer	110.00	65.00	65.00	25.00	110.00	60.00
Egg Cup, Footed	100.00	55.00	45.00	25.00	85.00	60.00
Hot Water Jug	525.00	225.00	200.00	120.00	450.00	225.00
Jam Pot w/Underliner	220.00	110.00	85.00	55.00	195.00	125.00
Milk Jug	525.00	225.00	175.00	120.00	425.00	200.00
Pin Tray	75.00	45.00	45.00	25.00	75.00	35.00
Plate, 6"	80.00	40.00	45.00	25.00	80.00	45.00
Plate, 9"	125.00	95.00	75.00	40.00	135.00	95.00
Plate, 10"	175.00	100.00	89.00	35.00	165.00	110.00
Relish	220.00	125.00	100.00	60.00	105.00	115.00
Salad Bowl (Chrome Rim)	225.00	110.00	110.00	60.00	175.00	125.00
Salt/Pepper on Tray	190.00	110.00	125.00	75.00	185.00	120.00
Sauce Boat, Underliner	150.00	105.00	100.00	65.00	150.00	115.00
Teacup and Saucer	125.00	60.00	70.00	40.00	125.00	60.00
Teapot, 2-cup	550.00	225.00	225.00	165.00	425.00	175.00
Teapot, 4-cup	725.00	325.00	300.00	180.00	650.00	325.00
Teapot, 6-cup	800.00	475.00	450.00	235.00	850.00	475.00
Teapot, Stacking	1050.00	500.00	625.00	300.00	950.00	500.00
Tennis Set	145.00	75.00	75.00	45.00	125.00	75.00
Toast Rack, 2-slice	200.00	135.00	125.00	85.00	200.00	120.00
Toast Rack, 4-slice	325.00	175.00	160.00	110.00	265.00	165.00
Trivet	120.00	75.00	75.00	50.00	100.00	75.00
Vase, Bud	150.00	95.00	85.00	50.00	150.00	105.00

COMPREHENSIVE PRICE GUIDE FOR CHINTZ

	CLOISONNE		CLYDE		COTSWOLD	
	U. S. $	U. K. £	U. S. $	U. K. £	U. S. $	U. K. £
Bedside, Breakfast Set	600.00	250.00	600.00	250.00	950.00	600.00
Bonbon	75.00	30.00	75.00	30.00	75.00	50.00
Bowl, 5"	85.00	45.00	85.00	45.00	65.00	40.00
Butter, Covered	150.00	75.00	150.00	75.00	225.00	110.00
Cake Plate, Open hdl.	125.00	70.00	125.00	70.00	165.00	80.00
Cake Plate, Pedestal	130.00	70.00	130.00	70.00	165.00	80.00
Cake Plate, Tiered	130.00	90.00	130.00	90.00	170.00	110.00
Candy/Sweets Dish	45.00	25.00	45.00	25.00	65.00	35.00
Cheese Keeper, Covd.	185.00	125.00	185.00	125.00	275.00	145.00
Coffee Pot	395.00	200.00	395.00	200.00	650.00	450.00
Compote	85.00	55.00	85.00	55.00	140.00	95.00
Condiment Set on Tray	140.00	85.00	140.00	85.00	210.00	150.00
Creamer and Sugar	75.00	50.00	75.00	50.00	140.00	100.00
Creamer/Sugar on Tray	125.00	70.00	125.00	70.00	225.00	140.00
Demitasse Cup/Saucer	65.00	25.00	65.00	25.00	95.00	55.00
Egg Cup, Footed	45.00	25.00	45.00	25.00	85.00	50.00
Hot Water Jug	200.00	120.00	200.00	120.00	395.00	225.00
Jam Pot w/Underliner	95.00	50.00	95.00	50.00	165.00	105.00
Milk Jug	175.00	110.00	175.00	110.00	395.00	200.00
Pin Tray	45.00	25.00	45.00	25.00	175.00	110.00
Plate, 6"	45.00	25.00	45.00	25.00	45.00	35.00
Plate, 9"	75.00	40.00	75.00	40.00	125.00	85.00
Plate, 10"	89.00	35.00	89.00	35.00	135.00	95.00
Relish	100.00	60.00	100.00	60.00	150.00	110.00
Salad Bowl (Chrome Rim)	110.00	60.00	110.00	60.00	155.00	110.00
Salt/Pepper on Tray	125.00	75.00	125.00	75.00	175.00	120.00
Sauce Boat, Underliner	100.00	65.00	100.00	65.00	145.00	115.00
Teacup and Saucer	75.00	45.00	75.00	45.00	135.00	75.00
Teapot, 2-cup	155.00	115.00	155.00	115.00	325.00	215.00
Teapot, 4-cup	250.00	120.00	250.00	120.00	425.00	275.00
Teapot, 6-cup	350.00	200.00	350.00	200.00	750.00	395.00
Teapot, Stacking	425.00	225.00	425.00	225.00	850.00	500.00
Tennis Set	75.00	45.00	75.00	45.00	125.00	70.00
Toast Rack, 2-slice	125.00	85.00	125.00	85.00	155.00	115.00
Toast Rack, 4-slice	160.00	110.00	160.00	110.00	225.00	140.00
Trivet	75.00	50.00	75.00	50.00	100.00	70.00
Vase, Bud	85.00	50.00	85.00	50.00	150.00	95.00

COMPREHENSIVE PRICE GUIDE FOR CHINTZ

	CRANSTONE		CROCUS		CROMER	
	U. S. $	U. K. £	U. S. $	U. K. £	U. S. $	U. K. £
Bedside, Breakfast Set	1350.00	650.00	950.00	600.00	600.00	325.00
Bonbon	135.00	95.00	85.00	45.00	45.00	30.00
Bowl, 5"	95.00	45.00	55.00	30.00	95.00	45.00
Butter, Covered	275.00	125.00	210.00	85.00	130.00	75.00
Cake Plate, Open hdl.	225.00	120.00	135.00	65.00	125.00	70.00
Cake Plate, Pedestal	265.00	170.00	165.00	80.00	130.00	70.00
Cake Plate, Tiered	265.00	190.00	170.00	110.00	130.00	90.00
Candy/Sweets Dish	95.00	55.00	65.00	35.00	45.00	25.00
Cheese Keeper, Covd.	300.00	175.00	265.00	135.00	450.00	275.00
Coffee Pot	950.00	600.00	650.00	300.00	450.00	310.00
Compote	225.00	150.00	140.00	95.00	140.00	85.00
Condiment Set on Tray	300.00	185.00	210.00	150.00	140.00	85.00
Creamer and Sugar	135.00	85.00	160.00	120.00	95.00	50.00
Creamer/Sugar on Tray	300.00	95.00	225.00	140.00	145.00	80.00
Demitasse Cup/Saucer	110.00	65.00	95.00	55.00	65.00	25.00
Egg Cup, Footed	100.00	65.00	85.00	50.00	45.00	25.00
Hot Water Jug	500.00	275.00	395.00	225.00	200.00	120.00
Jam Pot w/Underliner	200.00	150.00	165.00	105.00	85.00	55.00
Milk Jug	475.00	250.00	395.00	200.00	175.00	120.00
Pin Tray	95.00	50.00	95.00	35.00	45.00	25.00
Plate, 6"	85.00	45.00	45.00	35.00	45.00	25.00
Plate, 9"	135.00	75.00	60.00	40.00	75.00	40.00
Plate, 10"	195.00	85.00	85.00	60.00	89.00	35.00
Relish	195.00	95.00	125.00	75.00	100.00	60.00
Salad Bowl (Chrome Rim)	195.00	110.00	120.00	80.00	110.00	60.00
Salt/Pepper on Tray	225.00	150.00	175.00	120.00	125.00	75.00
Sauce Boat, Underliner	175.00	125.00	145.00	115.00	100.00	65.00
Teacup and Saucer	135.00	75.00	135.00	75.00	70.00	40.00
Teapot, 2-cup	350.00	200.00	325.00	215.00	225.00	165.00
Teapot, 4-cup	650.00	300.00	425.00	275.00	300.00	180.00
Teapot, 6-cup	950.00	500.00	750.00	395.00	450.00	235.00
Teapot, Stacking	1100.00	575.00	850.00	500.00	625.00	300.00
Tennis Set	145.00	95.00	125.00	70.00	75.00	45.00
Toast Rack, 2-slice	235.00	125.00	155.00	115.00	125.00	85.00
Toast Rack, 4-slice	295.00	155.00	225.00	140.00	160.00	110.00
Trivet	135.00	100.00	100.00	70.00	75.00	50.00
Vase, Bud	175.00	90.00	150.00	95.00	85.00	50.00

COMPREHENSIVE PRICE GUIDE FOR CHINTZ

	DELPHINIUM CHINTZ		DORSET		ELEANOR	
	U. S. $	U. K. £	U. S. $	U. K. £	U. S. $	U. K. £
Bedside, Breakfast Set	850.00	360.00	600.00	325.00	800.00	360.00
Bonbon	55.00	30.00	45.00	30.00	55.00	30.00
Bowl, 5"	65.00	35.00	95.00	45.00	65.00	35.00
Butter, Covered	225.00	85.00	125.00	75.00	225.00	85.00
Cake Plate, Open hdl.	135.00	85.00	125.00	70.00	135.00	85.00
Cake Plate, Pedestal	140.00	95.00	130.00	70.00	140.00	95.00
Cake Plate, Tiered	150.00	100.00	130.00	90.00	150.00	100.00
Candy/Sweets Dish	65.00	35.00	45.00	25.00	65.00	35.00
Cheese Keeper, Covd.	175.00	115.00	195.00	275.00	175.00	115.00
Coffee Pot	350.00	200.00	450.00	310.00	350.00	200.00
Compote	110.00	65.00	140.00	85.00	110.00	65.00
Condiment Set on Tray	150.00	100.00	140.00	85.00	150.00	100.00
Creamer and Sugar	100.00	60.00	95.00	50.00	100.00	60.00
Creamer/Sugar on Tray	150.00	100.00	145.00	80.00	150.00	100.00
Demitasse Cup/Saucer	75.00	45.00	65.00	25.00	75.00	45.00
Egg Cup, Footed	65.00	30.00	45.00	25.00	65.00	30.00
Hot Water Jug	275.00	150.00	200.00	120.00	275.00	150.00
Jam Pot w/Underliner	125.00	75.00	85.00	55.00	125.00	75.00
Milk Jug	250.00	125.00	175.00	120.00	250.00	125.00
Pin Tray	45.00	25.00	45.00	25.00	45.00	25.00
Plate, 6"	50.00	30.00	45.00	25.00	50.00	30.00
Plate, 9"	60.00	40.00	75.00	40.00	60.00	40.00
Plate, 10"	85.00	60.00	89.00	35.00	85.00	60.00
Relish	125.00	75.00	100.00	60.00	125.00	75.00
Salad Bowl (Chrome Rim)	105.00	60.00	110.00	60.00	105.00	60.00
Salt/Pepper on Tray	150.00	85.00	125.00	75.00	150.00	85.00
Sauce Boat, Underliner	115.00	70.00	100.00	65.00	115.00	70.00
Teacup and Saucer	80.00	45.00	65.00	33.00	80.00	45.00
Teapot, 2-cup	225.00	125.00	190.00	95.00	225.00	125.00
Teapot, 4-cup	350.00	200.00	290.00	130.00	350.00	200.00
Teapot, 6-cup	475.00	300.00	430.00	200.00	475.00	300.00
Teapot, Stacking	650.00	425.00	525.00	200.00	650.00	425.00
Tennis Set	85.00	50.00	65.00	40.00	85.00	50.00
Toast Rack, 2-slice	125.00	70.00	125.00	75.00	125.00	70.00
Toast Rack, 4-slice	185.00	120.00	185.00	120.00	185.00	120.00
Trivet	75.00	50.00	75.00	40.00	75.00	50.00
Vase, Bud	100.00	60.00	90.00	50.00	100.00	60.00

COMPREHENSIVE PRICE GUIDE FOR CHINTZ

	ENGLISH ROSE		ESTELLE		ESTHER	
	U.S. $	U.K. £	U.S. $	U.K. £	U.S. $	U.K. £
Bedside, Breakfast Set	1350.00	650.00	1110.00	600.00	1200.00	600.00
Bonbon	135.00	95.00	55.00	40.00	55.00	40.00
Bowl, 5"	95.00	45.00	55.00	40.00	65.00	40.00
Butter, Covered	275.00	125.00	175.00	95.00	235.00	135.00
Cake Plate, Open hdl.	225.00	120.00	145.00	85.00	225.00	150.00
Cake Plate, Pedestal	265.00	170.00	155.00	90.00	225.00	150.00
Cake Plate, Tiered	265.00	190.00	185.00	100.00	235.00	150.00
Candy/Sweets Dish	95.00	55.00	75.00	45.00	75.00	45.00
Cheese Keeper, Covd.	300.00	175.00	210.00	165.00	300.00	215.00
Coffee Pot	950.00	600.00	750.00	450.00	850.00	450.00
Compote	225.00	150.00	140.00	95.00	175.00	120.00
Condiment Set on Tray	300.00	185.00	215.00	120.00	265.00	140.00
Creamer and Sugar	135.00	85.00	125.00	75.00	155.00	95.00
Creamer/Sugar on Tray	300.00	95.00	200.00	140.00	275.00	170.00
Demitasse Cup/Saucer	110.00	65.00	70.00	50.00	110.00	60.00
Egg Cup, Footed	100.00	65.00	95.00	50.00	85.00	60.00
Hot Water Jug	500.00	275.00	400.00	185.00	450.00	225.00
Jam Pot w/Underliner	200.00	150.00	145.00	90.00	195.00	125.00
Milk Jug	475.00	250.00	325.00	165.00	425.00	200.00
Pin Tray	95.00	50.00	75.00	35.00	75.00	35.00
Plate, 6"	85.00	45.00	80.00	45.00	80.00	45.00
Plate, 9"	135.00	75.00	125.00	80.00	135.00	95.00
Plate, 10"	195.00	85.00	140.00	90.00	165.00	110.00
Relish	195.00	95.00	150.00	115.00	105.00	115.00
Salad Bowl (Chrome Rim)	195.00	110.00	165.00	90.00	175.00	125.00
Salt/Pepper on Tray	225.00	150.00	175.00	120.00	185.00	120.00
Sauce Boat, Underliner	175.00	125.00	130.00	105.00	150.00	115.00
Teacup and Saucer	135.00	75.00	125.00	60.00	125.00	60.00
Teapot, 2-cup	350.00	200.00	425.00	210.00	425.00	175.00
Teapot, 4-cup	650.00	300.00	550.00	315.00	650.00	325.00
Teapot, 6-cup	950.00	500.00	850.00	475.00	850.00	475.00
Teapot, Stacking	1100.00	575.00	950.00	500.00	950.00	500.00
Tennis Set	145.00	95.00	125.00	75.00	125.00	75.00
Toast Rack, 2-slice	235.00	125.00	175.00	105.00	200.00	120.00
Toast Rack, 4-slice	295.00	155.00	235.00	150.00	265.00	165.00
Trivet	135.00	100.00	90.00	65.00	100.00	75.00
Vase, Bud	175.00	90.00	135.00	75.00	150.00	105.00

COMPREHENSIVE PRICE GUIDE FOR CHINTZ

	EVESHAM		EXOTIC BIRD		BLACK FIREGLOW	
	U. S. $	U. K. £	U. S. $	U. K. £	U. S. $	U. K. £
Bedside, Breakfast Set	1450.00	650.00	800.00	360.00	490.00	250.00
Bonbon	115.00	75.00	55.00	30.00	45.00	20.00
Bowl, 5"	95.00	45.00	65.00	35.00	40.00	25.00
Butter, Covered	275.00	135.00	225.00	85.00	135.00	85.00
Cake Plate, Open hdl.	225.00	120.00	135.00	85.00	90.00	60.00
Cake Plate, Pedestal	265.00	130.00	140.00	95.00	100.00	60.00
Cake Plate, Tiered	295.00	195.00	150.00	100.00	110.00	65.00
Candy/Sweets Dish	95.00	55.00	65.00	35.00	40.00	25.00
Cheese Keeper, Covd.	335.00	275.00	175.00	115.00	145.00	95.00
Coffee Pot	950.00	600.00	350.00	200.00	375.00	210.00
Compote	225.00	150.00	110.00	65.00	75.00	45.00
Condiment Set on Tray	325.00	200.00	150.00	100.00	125.00	70.00
Creamer and Sugar	155.00	100.00	100.00	60.00	65.00	40.00
Creamer/Sugar on Tray	325.00	225.00	150.00	100.00	100.00	55.00
Demitasse Cup/Saucer	125.00	75.00	75.00	45.00	55.00	30.00
Egg Cup, Footed	100.00	65.00	65.00	30.00	40.00	25.00
Hot Water Jug	575.00	325.00	275.00	150.00	175.00	110.00
Jam Pot w/Underliner	235.00	130.00	125.00	75.00	95.00	60.00
Milk Jug	475.00	275.00	250.00	125.00	165.00	80.00
Pin Tray	95.00	50.00	45.00	25.00	40.00	25.00
Plate, 6"	85.00	45.00	50.00	30.00	45.00	25.00
Plate, 9"	135.00	75.00	60.00	40.00	65.00	45.00
Plate, 10"	195.00	85.00	85.00	60.00	75.00	50.00
Relish	225.00	95.00	125.00	75.00	75.00	55.00
Salad Bowl (Chrome Rim)	325.00	135.00	105.00	60.00	90.00	65.00
Salt/Pepper on Tray	235.00	150.00	150.00	85.00	100.00	70.00
Sauce Boat, Underliner	225.00	135.00	115.00	70.00	65.00	40.00
Teacup and Saucer	145.00	80.00	80.00	45.00	65.00	30.00
Teapot, 2-cup	550.00	295.00	225.00	125.00	150.00	100.00
Teapot, 4-cup	695.00	400.00	350.00	200.00	225.00	150.00
Teapot, 6-cup	950.00	600.00	475.00	300.00	375.00	210.00
Teapot, Stacking	1250.00	675.00	650.00	425.00	400.00	265.00
Tennis Set	155.00	95.00	85.00	50.00	55.00	35.00
Toast Rack, 2-slice	275.00	125.00	125.00	70.00	95.00	60.00
Toast Rack, 4-slice	365.00	195.00	185.00	120.00	150.00	110.00
Trivet	135.00	100.00	75.00	50.00	50.00	40.00
Vase, Bud	175.00	90.00	100.00	60.00	75.00	40.00

COMPREHENSIVE PRICE GUIDE FOR CHINTZ

	WHITE FIREGLOW		FLORAL FEAST		FLORAL GARDEN	
	U. S. $	U. K. £	U. S. $	U. K. £	U. S. $	U. K. £
Bedside, Breakfast Set	800.00	360.00	800.00	360.00	490.00	250.00
Bonbon	55.00	25.00	55.00	25.00	40.00	25.00
Bowl, 5"	65.00	35.00	65.00	35.00	40.00	25.00
Butter, Covered	225.00	85.00	225.00	85.00	135.00	85.00
Cake Plate, Open hdl.	135.00	85.00	135.00	85.00	90.00	60.00
Cake Plate, Pedestal	140.00	95.00	140.00	95.00	100.00	60.00
Cake Plate, Tiered	150.00	100.00	150.00	100.00	110.00	65.00
Candy/Sweets Dish	65.00	35.00	65.00	35.00	40.00	25.00
Cheese Keeper, Covd.	175.00	115.00	175.00	115.00	145.00	95.00
Coffee Pot	350.00	200.00	350.00	200.00	375.00	210.00
Compote	110.00	65.00	110.00	65.00	75.00	45.00
Condiment Set on Tray	150.00	100.00	150.00	100.00	125.00	70.00
Creamer and Sugar	100.00	60.00	100.00	60.00	65.00	40.00
Creamer/Sugar on Tray	150.00	100.00	150.00	100.00	100.00	55.00
Demitasse Cup/Saucer	75.00	45.00	75.00	45.00	55.00	30.00
Egg Cup, Footed	65.00	30.00	65.00	30.00	40.00	25.00
Hot Water Jug	275.00	150.00	275.00	150.00	175.00	110.00
Jam Pot w/Underliner	125.00	75.00	125.00	75.00	95.00	60.00
Milk Jug	250.00	125.00	250.00	125.00	165.00	80.00
Pin Tray	45.00	25.00	45.00	25.00	40.00	25.00
Plate, 6"	50.00	30.00	50.00	30.00	45.00	25.00
Plate, 9"	60.00	40.00	60.00	40.00	65.00	45.00
Plate, 10"	85.00	60.00	85.00	60.00	75.00	50.00
Relish	125.00	75.00	125.00	75.00	75.00	55.00
Salad Bowl (Chrome Rim)	105.00	60.00	105.00	60.00	90.00	65.00
Salt/Pepper on Tray	150.00	85.00	150.00	85.00	100.00	70.00
Sauce Boat, Underliner	115.00	70.00	115.00	70.00	65.00	40.00
Teacup and Saucer	80.00	45.00	80.00	45.00	55.00	30.00
Teapot, 2-cup	225.00	125.00	225.00	125.00	150.00	100.00
Teapot, 4-cup	350.00	200.00	350.00	200.00	225.00	150.00
Teapot, 6-cup	475.00	300.00	475.00	300.00	375.00	210.00
Teapot, Stacking	650.00	425.00	650.00	425.00	400.00	265.00
Tennis Set	85.00	50.00	85.00	50.00	55.00	35.00
Toast Rack, 2-slice	125.00	70.00	125.00	70.00	95.00	60.00
Toast Rack, 4-slice	185.00	120.00	185.00	120.00	150.00	110.00
Trivet	75.00	50.00	75.00	50.00	50.00	40.00
Vase, Bud	100.00	60.00	100.00	60.00	75.00	40.00

COMPREHENSIVE PRICE GUIDE FOR CHINTZ

	FLORENCE		HAZEL		JACOBEAN	
	U. S. $	U. K. £	U. S. $	U. K. £	U. S. $	U. K. £
Bedside, Breakfast Set	1450.00	650.00	1450.00	650.00	490.00	250.00
Bonbon	115.00	75.00	115.00	75.00	45.00	30.00
Bowl, 5"	95.00	45.00	95.00	45.00	40.00	25.00
Butter, Covered	275.00	135.00	275.00	135.00	135.00	85.00
Cake Plate, Open hdl.	225.00	120.00	225.00	120.00	90.00	60.00
Cake Plate, Pedestal	265.00	130.00	265.00	130.00	100.00	60.00
Cake Plate, Tiered	295.00	195.00	295.00	195.00	110.00	65.00
Candy/Sweets Dish	95.00	55.00	95.00	55.00	40.00	25.00
Cheese Keeper, Covd.	335.00	275.00	335.00	275.00	145.00	95.00
Coffee Pot	950.00	600.00	950.00	600.00	375.00	210.00
Compote	225.00	150.00	225.00	150.00	75.00	45.00
Condiment Set on Tray	325.00	200.00	325.00	200.00	125.00	70.00
Creamer and Sugar	155.00	100.00	155.00	100.00	65.00	40.00
Creamer/Sugar on Tray	325.00	225.00	325.00	225.00	100.00	55.00
Demitasse Cup/Saucer	125.00	75.00	125.00	75.00	55.00	30.00
Egg Cup, Footed	100.00	65.00	100.00	65.00	40.00	25.00
Hot Water Jug	575.00	325.00	575.00	325.00	175.00	110.00
Jam Pot w/Underliner	235.00	130.00	235.00	130.00	95.00	60.00
Milk Jug	475.00	275.00	475.00	275.00	165.00	80.00
Pin Tray	95.00	50.00	95.00	50.00	40.00	25.00
Plate, 6"	85.00	45.00	85.00	45.00	45.00	25.00
Plate, 9"	135.00	75.00	135.00	75.00	65.00	45.00
Plate, 10"	195.00	85.00	195.00	85.00	75.00	50.00
Relish	225.00	95.00	225.00	95.00	75.00	55.00
Salad Bowl (Chrome Rim)	325.00	135.00	325.00	135.00	90.00	65.00
Salt/Pepper on Tray	235.00	150.00	235.00	150.00	100.00	70.00
Sauce Boat, Underliner	225.00	135.00	225.00	135.00	65.00	40.00
Teacup and Saucer	145.00	80.00	145.00	80.00	55.00	30.00
Teapot, 2-cup	550.00	295.00	550.00	295.00	150.00	100.00
Teapot, 4-cup	695.00	400.00	695.00	400.00	225.00	150.00
Teapot, 6-cup	950.00	600.00	950.00	600.00	375.00	210.00
Teapot, Stacking	1250.00	675.00	1250.00	675.00	400.00	265.00
Tennis Set	155.00	95.00	155.00	95.00	55.00	35.00
Toast Rack, 2-slice	275.00	125.00	275.00	125.00	95.00	60.00
Toast Rack, 4-slice	365.00	195.00	365.00	195.00	150.00	110.00
Trivet	135.00	100.00	135.00	100.00	50.00	40.00
Vase, Bud	175.00	90.00	175.00	90.00	75.00	40.00

COMPREHENSIVE PRICE GUIDE FOR CHINTZ

	JACOBINA		JOYCE LYNN		JULIA	
	U. S. $	U. K. £	U. S. $	U. K. £	U. S. $	U. K. £
Bedside, Breakfast Set	490.00	250.00	1100.00	600.00	1650.00	800.00
Bonbon	40.00	20.00	115.00	50.00	135.00	95.00
Bowl, 5"	40.00	25.00	55.00	40.00	80.00	50.00
Butter, Covered	135.00	85.00	175.00	95.00	385.00	190.00
Cake Plate, Open hdl.	90.00	60.00	145.00	85.00	350.00	195.00
Cake Plate, Pedestal	100.00	60.00	155.00	90.00	375.00	195.00
Cake Plate, Tiered	110.00	65.00	185.00	100.00	400.00	195.00
Candy/Sweets Dish	40.00	25.00	75.00	45.00	100.00	50.00
Cheese Keeper, Covd.	145.00	95.00	210.00	165.00	395.00	225.00
Coffee Pot	375.00	210.00	75.00	450.00	1100.00	700.00
Compote	75.00	45.00	140.00	95.00	145.00	110.00
Condiment Set on Tray	125.00	70.00	215.00	120.00	375.00	225.00
Creamer and Sugar	65.00	40.00	125.00	75.00	205.00	150.00
Creamer/Sugar on Tray	100.00	55.00	200.00	140.00	410.00	290.00
Demitasse Cup/Saucer	55.00	30.00	70.00	50.00	130.00	95.00
Egg Cup, Footed	40.00	25.00	95.00	50.00	145.00	80.00
Hot Water Jug	175.00	110.00	400.00	185.00	825.00	450.00
Jam Pot w/Underliner	95.00	60.00	145.00	90.00	415.00	300.00
Milk Jug	165.00	80.00	325.00	165.00	625.00	355.00
Pin Tray	40.00	25.00	75.00	35.00	95.00	60.00
Plate, 6"	45.00	25.00	80.00	45.00	140.00	95.00
Plate, 9"	65.00	45.00	125.00	80.00	225.00	140.00
Plate, 10"	75.00	50.00	140.00	90.00	250.00	150.00
Relish	75.00	55.00	150.00	115.00	310.00	225.00
Salad Bowl (Chrome Rim)	90.00	65.00	165.00	90.00	345.00	225.00
Salt/Pepper on Tray	100.00	70.00	175.00	120.00	295.00	190.00
Sauce Boat, Underliner	65.00	40.00	130.00	105.00	275.00	185.00
Teacup and Saucer	55.00	30.00	125.00	60.00	195.00	95.00
Teapot, 2-cup	150.00	100.00	425.00	210.00	750.00	535.00
Teapot, 4-cup	225.00	150.00	550.00	315.00	950.00	700.00
Teapot, 6-cup	375.00	210.00	850.00	475.00	1250.00	800.00
Teapot, Stacking	400.00	265.00	950.00	500.00	1500.00	850.00
Tennis Set	55.00	35.00	125.00	75.00	245.00	120.00
Toast Rack, 2-slice	95.00	60.00	175.00	105.00	310.00	220.00
Toast Rack, 4-slice	150.00	110.00	235.00	150.00	375.00	250.00
Trivet	50.00	40.00	90.00	65.00	195.00	140.00
Vase, Bud	75.00	40.00	135.00	75.00	225.00	150.00

COMPREHENSIVE PRICE GUIDE FOR CHINTZ

	JUNE FESTIVAL		JUNE ROSES		KEW	
	U.S. $	U.K. £	U.S. $	U.K. £	U.S. $	U.K. £
Bedside, Breakfast Set	800.00	360.00	1350.00	650.00	85 0.00	360.00
Bonbon	60.00	25.00	135.00	95.00	60.00	20.00
Bowl, 5"	65.00	35.00	95.00	45.00	65.00	35.00
Butter, Covered	225.00	85.00	275.00	125.00	225.00	85.00
Cake Plate, Open hdl.	135.00	85.00	225.00	120.00	135.00	85.00
Cake Plate, Pedestal	140.00	95.00	265.00	170.00	140.00	95.00
Cake Plate, Tiered	150.00	100.00	265.00	190.00	150.00	100.00
Candy/Sweets Dish	65.00	35.00	95.00	55.00	65.00	35.00
Cheese Keeper, Covd.	175.00	115.00	300.00	175.00	175.00	115.00
Coffee Pot	350.00	200.00	950.00	600.00	350.00	200.00
Compote	110.00	65.00	225.00	150.00	110.00	65.00
Condiment Set on Tray	150.00	100.00	300.00	185.00	150.00	100.00
Creamer and Sugar	100.00	60.00	135.00	85.00	100.00	60.00
Creamer/Sugar on Tray	150.00	100.00	300.00	95.00	150.00	100.00
Demitasse Cup/Saucer	75.00	45.00	110.00	65.00	75.00	45.00
Egg Cup, Footed	65.00	30.00	100.00	65.00	65.00	30.00
Hot Water Jug	275.00	150.00	500.00	275.00	275.00	150.00
Jam Pot w/Underliner	125.00	75.00	200.00	150.00	125.00	75.00
Milk Jug	250.00	125.00	475.00	250.00	250.00	125.00
Pin Tray	45.00	25.00	95.00	50.00	65.00	25.00
Plate, 6"	50.00	30.00	85.00	45.00	60.00	30.00
Plate, 9"	60.00	40.00	135.00	75.00	60.00	40.00
Plate, 10"	85.00	60.00	195.00	85.00	85.00	60.00
Relish	125.00	75.00	195.00	95.00	125.00	75.00
Salad Bowl (Chrome Rim)	105.00	60.00	195.00	110.00	105.00	60.00
Salt/Pepper on Tray	150.00	85.00	225.00	150.00	150.00	85.00
Sauce Boat, Underliner	115.00	70.00	175.00	125.00	115.00	70.00
Teacup and Saucer	80.00	45.00	135.00	75.00	80.00	45.00
Teapot, 2-cup	225.00	125.00	350.00	200.00	225.00	125.00
Teapot, 4-cup	350.00	200.00	650.00	300.00	350.00	200.00
Teapot, 6-cup	475.00	300.00	950.00	500.00	475.00	300.00
Teapot, Stacking	650.00	425.00	1100.00	575.00	650.00	425.00
Tennis Set	85.00	50.00	145.00	95.00	85.00	50.00
Toast Rack, 2-slice	125.00	70.00	235.00	125.00	125.00	70.00
Toast Rack, 4-slice	185.00	120.00	295.00	155.00	185.00	120.00
Trivet	75.00	50.00	135.00	100.00	75.00	50.00
Vase, Bud	100.00	60.00	175.00	90.00	100.00	60.00

COMPREHENSIVE PRICE GUIDE FOR CHINTZ

	KINVER		MAJESTIC		MARGUERITE	
	U. S. $	U. K. £	U. S. $	U. K. £	U. S. $	U. K. £
Bedside, Breakfast Set	1350.00	650.00	1350.00	650.00	750.00	350.00
Bonbon	135.00	95.00	135.00	95.00	55.00	35.00
Bowl, 5"	95.00	45.00	95.00	45.00	60.00	25.00
Butter, Covered	275.00	125.00	275.00	125.00	175.00	85.00
Cake Plate, Open hdl.	225.00	120.00	225.00	120.00	125.00	85.00
Cake Plate, Pedestal	265.00	170.00	265.00	170.00	135.00	95.00
Cake Plate, Tiered	265.00	190.00	265.00	190.00	145.00	100.00
Candy/Sweets Dish	95.00	55.00	95.00	55.00	55.00	35.00
Cheese Keeper, Covd.	300.00	175.00	300.00	175.00	195.00	115.00
Coffee Pot	950.00	600.00	950.00	600.00	375.00	210.00
Compote	225.00	150.00	225.00	150.00	85.00	60.00
Condiment Set on Tray	300.00	185.00	300.00	185.00	140.00	100.00
Creamer and Sugar	135.00	85.00	135.00	85.00	95.00	55.00
Creamer/Sugar on Tray	300.00	95.00	300.00	95.00	135.00	80.00
Demitasse Cup/Saucer	110.00	65.00	110.00	65.00	65.00	40.00
Egg Cup, Footed	100.00	65.00	100.00	65.00	65.00	30.00
Hot Water Jug	500.00	275.00	500.00	275.00	200.00	130.00
Jam Pot w/Underliner	200.00	150.00	200.00	150.00	100.00	45.00
Milk Jug	475.00	250.00	475.00	250.00	175.00	110.00
Pin Tray	95.00	50.00	95.00	50.00	45.00	25.00
Plate, 6"	85.00	45.00	85.00	45.00	50.00	30.00
Plate, 9"	135.00	75.00	135.00	75.00	85.00	45.00
Plate, 10"	195.00	85.00	195.00	85.00	105.00	65.00
Relish	195.00	95.00	195.00	95.00	120.00	65.00
Salad Bowl (Chrome Rim)	195.00	110.00	195.00	110.00	105.00	60.00
Salt/Pepper on Tray	225.00	150.00	225.00	150.00	135.00	85.00
Sauce Boat, Underliner	175.00	125.00	175.00	125.00	105.00	60.00
Teacup and Saucer	135.00	75.00	135.00	75.00	75.00	45.00
Teapot, 2-cup	350.00	200.00	350.00	200.00	175.00	110.00
Teapot, 4-cup	650.00	300.00	650.00	300.00	295.00	125.00
Teapot, 6-cup	950.00	500.00	950.00	500.00	450.00	225.00
Teapot, Stacking	1100.00	575.00	1100.00	575.00	625.00	300.00
Tennis Set	145.00	95.00	145.00	95.00	85.00	50.00
Toast Rack, 2-slice	235.00	125.00	235.00	125.00	125.00	70.00
Toast Rack, 4-slice	295.00	155.00	295.00	155.00	175.00	90.00
Trivet	135.00	100.00	135.00	100.00	65.00	45.00
Vase, Bud	175.00	90.00	175.00	90.00	85.00	50.00

COMPREHENSIVE PRICE GUIDE FOR CHINTZ

	MARION		MAYFAIR		MAY FESTIVAL	
	U. S. $	**U. K. £**	**U. S. $**	**U. K. £**	**U. S. $**	**U. K. £**
Bedside, Breakfast Set	1100.00	650.00	1000.00	650.00	800.00	360.00
Bonbon	95.00	60.00	85.00	40.00	60.00	25.00
Bowl, 5"	70.00	40.00	70.00	40.00	65.00	35.00
Butter, Covered	325.00	125.00	325.00	135.00	225.00	85.00
Cake Plate, Open hdl.	200.00	140.00	200.00	140.00	135.00	85.00
Cake Plate, Pedestal	210.00	150.00	210.00	150.00	140.00	95.00
Cake Plate, Tiered	225.00	155.00	225.00	155.00	150.00	100.00
Candy/Sweets Dish	110.00	55.00	110.00	55.00	65.00	35.00
Cheese Keeper, Covd.	250.00	175.00	250.00	165.00	175.00	115.00
Coffee Pot	850.00	600.00	850.00	575.00	350.00	200.00
Compote	175.00	120.00	175.00	120.00	110.00	65.00
Condiment Set on Tray	225.00	145.00	225.00	145.00	150.00	100.00
Creamer and Sugar	135.00	85.00	135.00	85.00	100.00	60.00
Creamer/Sugar on Tray	235.00	145.00	235.00	145.00	150.00	100.00
Demitasse Cup/Saucer	110.00	60.00	110.00	60.00	75.00	45.00
Egg Cup, Footed	90.00	50.00	90.00	50.00	65.00	30.00
Hot Water Jug	465.00	255.00	465.00	255.00	275.00	150.00
Jam Pot w/Underliner	195.00	130.00	195.00	130.00	125.00	75.00
Milk Jug	450.00	210.00	450.00	210.00	250.00	125.00
Pin Tray	85.00	40.00	85.00	40.00	45.00	25.00
Plate, 6"	85.00	40.00	90.00	40.00	50.00	30.00
Plate, 9"	145.00	75.00	145.00	75.00	60.00	40.00
Plate, 10"	169.00	85.00	165.00	95.00	85.00	60.00
Relish	185.00	110.00	185.00	125.00	125.00	75.00
Salad Bowl (Chrome Rim)	185.00	110.00	185.00	110.00	105.00	60.00
Salt/Pepper on Tray	155.00	110.00	155.00	110.00	150.00	85.00
Sauce Boat, Underliner	165.00	115.00	175.00	120.00	115.00	70.00
Teacup and Saucer	125.00	70.00	125.00	70.00	80.00	45.00
Teapot, 2-cup	350.00	200.00	350.00	200.00	225.00	125.00
Teapot, 4-cup	650.00	325.00	650.00	325.00	350.00	200.00
Teapot, 6-cup	850.00	450.00	850.00	450.00	475.00	300.00
Teapot, Stacking	950.00	525.00	950.00	525.00	650.00	425.00
Tennis Set	125.00	75.00	125.00	75.00	85.00	50.00
Toast Rack, 2-slice	185.00	105.00	185.00	105.00	125.00	70.00
Toast Rack, 4-slice	235.00	135.00	235.00	135.00	185.00	120.00
Trivet	125.00	80.00	125.00	80.00	75.00	50.00
Vase, Bud	150.00	90.00	150.00	90.00	100.00	60.00

COMPREHENSIVE PRICE GUIDE FOR CHINTZ

	MINTON		MORNING GLORY		NANTWICH	
	U. S. $	U. K. £	U. S. $	U. K. £	U. S. $	U. K. £
Beaker	45.00	25.00				
Bedside, Breakfast Set			850.00	360.00	1250.00	500.00
Bonbon	50.00	25.00	45.00	25.00	80.00	40.00
Bowl, 5"			65.00	35.00	85.00	40.00
Butter, Covered			225.00	85.00	195.00	135.00
Cake Plate, Open hdl.			135.00	85.00	165.00	130.00
Cake Plate, Pedestal			140.00	95.00	170.00	130.00
Cake Plate, Tiered			150.00	100.00	180.00	140.00
Candy/Sweets Dish	40.00	20.00	65.00	35.00	75.00	35.00
Cheese Keeper, Covd.			175.00	115.00	235.00	170.00
Coffee Pot			350.00	200.00	850.00	375.00
Compote			110.00	65.00	159.00	120.00
Condiment Set on Tray			150.00	100.00	225.00	140.00
Creamer and Sugar			100.00	60.00	165.00	95.00
Creamer/Sugar on Tray			150.00	100.00	225.00	170.00
Demitasse Cup/Saucer			75.00	45.00	95.00	50.00
Egg Cup, Footed			65.00	30.00	85.00	60.00
Hot Water Jug			275.00	150.00	225.00	125.00
Jam Pot w/Underliner			125.00	75.00	175.00	110.00
Mayo Dish w/Lid	165.00	85.00				
Milk Jug			250.00	125.00	425.00	200.00
Pin Tray			45.00	25.00	75.00	35.00
Plate, 6"	35.00	15.00	50.00	30.00	85.00	40.00
Plate, 9"	45.00	20.00	60.00	40.00	135.00	95.00
Plate, 10"			85.00	60.00	155.00	100.00
Relish			125.00	75.00	175.00	110.00
Salad Bowl (Chrome Rim)			105.00	60.00	150.00	115.00
Salt/Pepper on Tray			150.00	85.00	185.00	120.00
Sauce Boat, Underliner			115.00	70.00	150.00	115.00
Teacup and Saucer			80.00	45.00	125.00	60.00
Teapot, 2-cup			225.00	125.00	425.00	175.00
Teapot, 4-cup			350.00	200.00	650.00	325.00
Teapot, 6-cup			475.00	300.00	850.00	475.00
Teapot, Stacking			650.00	425.00	950.00	500.00
Tennis Set			85.00	50.00	125.00	75.00
Toast Rack, 2-slice			125.00	70.00	165.00	120.00
Toast Rack, 4-slice			185.00	120.00	200.00	165.00
Trivet			75.00	50.00	100.00	75.00
Vase, Bud			100.00	60.00	150.00	105.00

COMPREHENSIVE PRICE GUIDE FOR CHINTZ

	OLD COTTAGE		ORIENT		PAISLEY	
	U. S. $	U. K. £	U. S. $	U. K. £	U. S. $	U. K. £
Bedside, Breakfast Set	850.00	360.00	500.00	225.00	500.00	250.00
Bonbon	85.00	50.00	45.00	25.00	45.00	25.00
Bowl, 5"	65.00	35.00	40.00	25.00	40.00	25.00
Butter, Covered	225.00	85.00	225.00	85.00	135.00	85.00
Cake Plate, Open hdl.	135.00	85.00	90.00	60.00	90.00	60.00
Cake Plate, Pedestal	140.00	95.00	100.00	60.00	100.00	60.00
Cake Plate, Tiered	150.00	100.00	110.00	65.00	110.00	65.00
Candy/Sweets Dish	65.00	35.00	40.00	25.00	40.00	25.00
Cheese Keeper, Covd.	175.00	115.00	145.00	95.00	145.00	95.00
Coffee Pot	350.00	200.00	375.00	210.00	375.00	210.00
Compote	110.00	65.00	75.00	45.00	75.00	45.00
Condiment Set on Tray	150.00	100.00	125.00	70.00	125.00	70.00
Creamer and Sugar	100.00	60.00	65.00	40.00	65.00	40.00
Creamer/Sugar on Tray	150.00	100.00	100.00	55.00	100.00	55.00
Demitasse Cup/Saucer	75.00	45.00	55.00	30.00	55.00	30.00
Egg Cup, Footed	65.00	30.00	40.00	25.00	40.00	25.00
Hot Water Jug	275.00	150.00	175.00	110.00	175.00	110.00
Jam Pot w/Underliner	125.00	75.00	95.00	60.00	95.00	60.00
Milk Jug	250.00	125.00	165.00	80.00	165.00	80.00
Pin Tray	45.00	25.00	40.00	25.00	40.00	25.00
Plate, 6"	50.00	30.00	45.00	25.00	45.00	25.00
Plate, 9"	60.00	40.00	65.00	45.00	65.00	45.00
Plate, 10"	85.00	60.00	75.00	50.00	75.00	50.00
Relish	125.00	75.00	75.00	55.00	75.00	55.00
Salad Bowl (Chrome Rim)	105.00	60.00	95.00	60.00	90.00	65.00
Salt/Pepper on Tray	150.00	85.00	100.00	70.00	100.00	70.00
Sauce Boat, Underliner	115.00	70.00	65.00	40.00	65.00	40.00
Teacup and Saucer	80.00	45.00	75.00	35.00	55.00	30.00
Teapot, 2-cup	225.00	125.00	165.00	100.00	150.00	100.00
Teapot, 4-cup	350.00	200.00	245.00	150.00	225.00	150.00
Teapot, 6-cup	475.00	300.00	395.00	210.00	375.00	210.00
Teapot, Stacking	650.00	425.00	450.00	245.00	400.00	265.00
Tennis Set	85.00	50.00	75.00	35.00	55.00	35.00
Toast Rack, 2-slice	125.00	70.00	95.00	60.00	95.00	60.00
Toast Rack, 4-slice	185.00	120.00	150.00	110.00	150.00	110.00
Trivet	75.00	50.00	50.00	40.00	50.00	40.00
Vase, Bud	100.00	60.00	75.00	40.00	75.00	35.00

COMPREHENSIVE PRICE GUIDE FOR CHINTZ

	PEBBLES		PEKIN		PELHAM	
	U. S. $	U. K. £	U. S. $	U. K. £	U. S. $	U. K. £
Bedside, Breakfast Set	490.00	250.00	550.00	250.00	750.00	325.00
Bonbon	45.00	30.00	45.00	30.00	75.00	45.00
Bowl, 5"	40.00	25.00	45.00	25.00	55.00	30.00
Butter, Covered	135.00	85.00	225.00	100.00	175.00	75.00
Cake Plate, Open hdl.	90.00	60.00	100.00	60.00	135.00	75.00
Cake Plate, Pedestal	100.00	60.00	110.00	65.00	150.00	95.00
Cake Plate, Tiered	110.00	65.00	125.00	75.00	165.00	100.00
Candy/Sweets Dish	40.00	25.00	45.00	25.00	55.00	30.00
Cheese Keeper, Covd.	145.00	95.00	210.00	110.00	185.00	115.00
Coffee Pot	375.00	210.00	395.00	200.00	450.00	200.00
Compote	75.00	45.00	75.00	45.00	100.00	65.00
Condiment Set on Tray	125.00	70.00	135.00	75.00	150.00	90.00
Creamer and Sugar	65.00	40.00	65.00	40.00	110.00	60.00
Creamer/Sugar on Tray	100.00	55.00	135.00	85.00	160.00	100.00
Demitasse Cup/Saucer	55.00	30.00	55.00	30.00	65.00	35.00
Egg Cup, Footed	40.00	25.00	45.00	25.00	65.00	30.00
Hot Water Jug	175.00	110.00	195.00	110.00	300.00	150.00
Jam Pot w/Underliner	95.00	60.00	95.00	55.00	125.00	75.00
Milk Jug	165.00	80.00	185.00	80.00	250.00	125.00
Pin Tray	40.00	25.00	45.00	25.00	50.00	25.00
Plate, 6"	45.00	25.00	50.00	25.00	50.00	25.00
Plate, 9"	65.00	45.00	75.00	45.00	95.00	45.00
Plate, 10"	75.00	50.00	95.00	50.00	125.00	60.00
Relish	75.00	55.00	95.00	50.00	125.00	70.00
Salad Bowl (Chrome Rim)	90.00	65.00	125.00	65.00	125.00	65.00
Salt/Pepper on Tray	100.00	70.00	100.00	50.00	145.00	85.00
Sauce Boat, Underliner	65.00	40.00	70.00	40.00	115.00	70.00
Teacup and Saucer	55.00	30.00	75.00	30.00	80.00	40.00
Teapot, 2-cup	150.00	100.00	140.00	90.00	225.00	125.00
Teapot, 4-cup	225.00	150.00	225.00	150.00	350.00	200.00
Teapot, 6-cup	375.00	210.00	375.00	210.00	475.00	300.00
Teapot, Stacking	400.00	265.00	450.00	250.00	600.00	400.00
Tennis Set	55.00	35.00	70.00	40.00	85.00	50.00
Toast Rack, 2-slice	95.00	60.00	110.00	50.00	150.00	70.00
Toast Rack, 4-slice	150.00	110.00	170.00	110.00	195.00	120.00
Trivet	50.00	40.00	50.00	40.00	75.00	50.00
Vase, Bud	75.00	40.00	75.00	40.00	110.00	50.00

COMPREHENSIVE PRICE GUIDE FOR CHINTZ

	PEONY		QUEEN ANNE		QUILT	
	U. S. $	U. K. £	U. S. $	U. K. £	U. S. $	U. K. £
Bedside, Breakfast Set	800.00	360.00	550.00	250.00	550.00	250.00
Bonbon	80.00	45.00	45.00	30.00	45.00	30.00
Bowl, 5"	65.00	35.00	45.00	25.00	45.00	25.00
Butter, Covered	225.00	85.00	225.00	100.00	225.00	100.00
Cake Plate, Open hdl.	135.00	85.00	100.00	60.00	100.00	60.00
Cake Plate, Pedestal	140.00	95.00	110.00	65.00	110.00	65.00
Cake Plate, Tiered	150.00	100.00	125.00	75.00	125.00	75.00
Candy/Sweets Dish	65.00	35.00	45.00	25.00	45.00	25.00
Cheese Keeper, Covd.	175.00	115.00	210.00	110.00	210.00	110.00
Coffee Pot	350.00	200.00	395.00	200.00	395.00	200.00
Compote	110.00	65.00	75.00	45.00	75.00	45.00
Condiment Set on Tray	150.00	100.00	135.00	75.00	135.00	75.00
Creamer and Sugar	100.00	60.00	65.00	40.00	65.00	40.00
Creamer/Sugar on Tray	150.00	100.00	135.00	85.00	135.00	85.00
Demitasse Cup/Saucer	75.00	45.00	55.00	30.00	55.00	30.00
Egg Cup, Footed	65.00	30.00	45.00	25.00	45.00	25.00
Hot Water Jug	275.00	150.00	195.00	110.00	195.00	110.00
Jam Pot w/Underliner	125.00	75.00	95.00	55.00	95.00	55.00
Milk Jug	250.00	125.00	185.00	80.00	185.00	80.00
Pin Tray	45.00	25.00	45.00	25.00	45.00	25.00
Plate, 6"	50.00	30.00	50.00	25.00	50.00	25.00
Plate, 9"	60.00	40.00	75.00	45.00	75.00	45.00
Plate, 10"	85.00	60.00	95.00	50.00	95.00	50.00
Relish	125.00	75.00	95.00	50.00	95.00	50.00
Salad Bowl (Chrome Rim)	105.00	60.00	125.00	65.00	125.00	65.00
Salt/Pepper on Tray	150.00	85.00	100.00	50.00	100.00	50.00
Sauce Boat, Underliner	115.00	70.00	70.00	40.00	70.00	40.00
Teacup and Saucer	80.00	45.00	75.00	30.00	75.00	30.00
Teapot, 2-cup	225.00	125.00	140.00	90.00	140.00	90.00
Teapot, 4-cup	350.00	200.00	225.00	150.00	225.00	150.00
Teapot, 6-cup	475.00	300.00	375.00	210.00	375.00	210.00
Teapot, Stacking	650.00	425.00	450.00	250.00	450.00	250.00
Tennis Set	85.00	50.00	70.00	40.00	70.00	40.00
Toast Rack, 2-slice	125.00	70.00	110.00	50.00	110.00	50.00
Toast Rack, 4-slice	185.00	120.00	170.00	110.00	170.00	110.00
Trivet	75.00	50.00	50.00	40.00	50.00	40.00
Vase, Bud	100.00	60.00	75.00	40.00	75.00	40.00

COMPREHENSIVE PRICE GUIDE FOR CHINTZ

	RICHMOND		ROSALIND		ROSE DU BARRY	
	U. S. $	U. K. £	U. S. $	U. K. £	U. S. $	U. K. £
Bedside, Breakfast Set	850.00	360.00	425.00	250.00	750.00	325.00
Bonbon	75.00	30.00	40.00	25.00	65.00	30.00
Bowl, 5"	65.00	35.00	40.00	25.00	55.00	30.00
Butter, Covered	225.00	85.00	135.00	85.00	175.00	75.00
Cake Plate, Open hdl.	135.00	85.00	90.00	60.00	135.00	75.00
Cake Plate, Pedestal	140.00	95.00	100.00	60.00	150.00	95.00
Cake Plate, Tiered	150.00	100.00	110.00	65.00	165.00	100.00
Candy/Sweets Dish	65.00	35.00	40.00	25.00	55.00	30.00
Cheese Keeper, Covd.	175.00	115.00	145.00	95.00	185.00	115.00
Coffee Pot	350.00	200.00	375.00	210.00	450.00	200.00
Compote	110.00	65.00	75.00	45.00	100.00	65.00
Condiment Set on Tray	150.00	100.00	125.00	70.00	150.00	90.00
Creamer and Sugar	100.00	60.00	65.00	40.00	110.00	60.00
Creamer/Sugar on Tray	150.00	100.00	100.00	55.00	160.00	100.00
Demitasse Cup/Saucer	75.00	45.00	55.00	30.00	65.00	35.00
Egg Cup, Footed	65.00	30.00	40.00	25.00	65.00	30.00
Hot Water Jug	275.00	150.00	175.00	110.00	300.00	150.00
Jam Pot w/Underliner	125.00	75.00	95.00	60.00	125.00	75.00
Milk Jug	250.00	125.00	165.00	80.00	250.00	125.00
Pin Tray	45.00	25.00	40.00	25.00	50.00	25.00
Plate, 6"	50.00	30.00	45.00	25.00	50.00	25.00
Plate, 9"	60.00	40.00	65.00	45.00	95.00	45.00
Plate, 10"	85.00	60.00	75.00	50.00	125.00	60.00
Relish	125.00	75.00	75.00	55.00	125.00	70.00
Salad Bowl (Chrome Rim)	105.00	60.00	90.00	65.00	125.00	65.00
Salt/Pepper on Tray	150.00	85.00	100.00	70.00	145.00	85.00
Sauce Boat, Underliner	115.00	70.00	65.00	40.00	115.00	70.00
Teacup and Saucer	80.00	45.00	55.00	30.00	80.00	40.00
Teapot, 2-cup	225.00	125.00	150.00	100.00	225.00	125.00
Teapot, 4-cup	350.00	200.00	225.00	150.00	350.00	200.00
Teapot, 6-cup	475.00	300.00	375.00	210.00	475.00	300.00
Teapot, Stacking	650.00	425.00	400.00	265.00	600.00	400.00
Tennis Set	85.00	50.00	55.00	35.00	85.00	50.00
Toast Rack, 2-slice	125.00	70.00	95.00	60.00	150.00	70.00
Toast Rack, 4-slice	185.00	120.00	150.00	110.00	195.00	120.00
Trivet	75.00	50.00	50.00	40.00	75.00	50.00
Vase, Bud	100.00	60.00	75.00	40.00	110.00	50.00

COMPREHENSIVE PRICE GUIDE FOR CHINTZ

	ROSE SPRIG		ROYALTY		RUTLAND	
	U.S. $	U.K. £	U.S. $	U.K. £	U.S. $	U.K. £
Bedside, Breakfast Set	1250.00	500.00	1300.00	700.00	800.00	360.00
Bonbon	80.00	50.00	95.00	50.00	75.00	35.00
Bowl, 5"	85.00	40.00	85.00	40.00	65.00	35.00
Butter, Covered	195.00	135.00	325.00	125.00	225.00	85.00
Cake Plate, Open hdl.	165.00	130.00	225.00	130.00	135.00	85.00
Cake Plate, Pedestal	170.00	130.00	250.00	130.00	140.00	95.00
Cake Plate, Tiered	180.00	140.00	265.00	140.00	150.00	100.00
Candy/Sweets Dish	75.00	35.00	75.00	35.00	65.00	35.00
Cheese Keeper, Covd.	235.00	170.00	325.00	225.00	175.00	115.00
Coffee Pot	850.00	375.00	1050.00	650.00	350.00	200.00
Compote	159.00	120.00	300.00	125.00	110.00	65.00
Condiment Set on Tray	225.00	140.00	275.00	145.00	150.00	100.00
Creamer and Sugar	165.00	95.00	135.00	95.00	100.00	60.00
Creamer/Sugar on Tray	225.00	170.00	275.00	150.00	150.00	100.00
Demitasse Cup/Saucer	95.00	50.00	110.00	65.00	75.00	45.00
Egg Cup, Footed	85.00	60.00	100.00	55.00	65.00	30.00
Hot Water Jug	225.00	125.00	525.00	225.00	275.00	150.00
Jam Pot w/Underliner	175.00	110.00	225.00	125.00	125.00	75.00
Milk Jug	425.00	200.00	525.00	225.00	250.00	125.00
Pin Tray	75.00	35.00	75.00	45.00	45.00	25.00
Plate, 6"	85.00	40.00	85.00	40.00	50.00	30.00
Plate, 9"	135.00	95.00	125.00	95.00	60.00	40.00
Plate, 10"	155.00	100.00	165.00	100.00	85.00	60.00
Relish	175.00	110.00	225.00	125.00	125.00	75.00
Salad Bowl (Chrome Rim)	150.00	115.00	250.00	125.00	105.00	60.00
Salt/Pepper on Tray	185.00	120.00	225.00	135.00	150.00	85.00
Sauce Boat, Underliner	150.00	115.00	200.00	115.00	115.00	70.00
Teacup and Saucer	125.00	60.00	125.00	60.00	80.00	45.00
Teapot, 2-cup	425.00	175.00	550.00	225.00	225.00	125.00
Teapot, 4-cup	650.00	325.00	725.00	325.00	350.00	200.00
Teapot, 6-cup	850.00	475.00	800.00	475.00	475.00	300.00
Teapot, Stacking	950.00	500.00	1200.00	500.00	650.00	425.00
Tennis Set	125.00	75.00	145.00	75.00	85.00	50.00
Toast Rack, 2-slice	165.00	120.00	220.00	135.00	125.00	70.00
Toast Rack, 4-slice	200.00	165.00	325.00	195.00	185.00	120.00
Trivet	100.00	75.00	140.00	95.00	75.00	50.00
Vase, Bud	150.00	105.00	175.00	100.00	100.00	60.00

COMPREHENSIVE PRICE GUIDE FOR CHINTZ

	SAMPLER		SHREWSBURY		SOMERSET	
	U. S. $	U. K. £	U. S. $	U. K. £	U. S. $	U. K. £
Bedside, Breakfast Set	750.00	325.00	1100.00	650.00	1350.00	650.00
Bonbon	55.00	30.00	95.00	60.00	135.00	95.00
Bowl, 5"	55.00	30.00	70.00	40.00	95.00	45.00
Butter, Covered	175.00	75.00	325.00	125.00	275.00	125.00
Cake Plate, Open hdl.	135.00	75.00	200.00	140.00	225.00	120.00
Cake Plate, Pedestal	150.00	95.00	210.00	150.00	265.00	170.00
Cake Plate, Tiered	165.00	100.00	225.00	155.00	265.00	190.00
Candy/Sweets Dish	55.00	30.00	110.00	55.00	95.00	55.00
Cheese Keeper, Covd.	185.00	115.00	250.00	175.00	300.00	175.00
Coffee Pot	450.00	200.00	850.00	600.00	950.00	600.00
Compote	100.00	65.00	175.00	120.00	225.00	150.00
Condiment Set on Tray	150.00	90.00	225.00	145.00	300.00	185.00
Creamer and Sugar	110.00	60.00	135.00	85.00	135.00	85.00
Creamer/Sugar on Tray	160.00	100.00	235.00	145.00	300.00	95.00
Demitasse Cup/Saucer	65.00	35.00	110.00	60.00	110.00	65.00
Egg Cup, Footed	65.00	30.00	90.00	50.00	100.00	65.00
Hot Water Jug	300.00	150.00	465.00	255.00	500.00	275.00
Jam Pot w/Underliner	125.00	75.00	195.00	130.00	200.00	150.00
Milk Jug	250.00	125.00	450.00	210.00	475.00	250.00
Pin Tray	50.00	25.00	85.00	40.00	95.00	50.00
Plate, 6"	50.00	25.00	85.00	40.00	85.00	45.00
Plate, 9"	95.00	45.00	145.00	75.00	135.00	75.00
Plate, 10"	125.00	60.00	169.00	85.00	195.00	85.00
Relish	125.00	70.00	185.00	110.00	195.00	95.00
Salad Bowl (Chrome Rim)	125.00	65.00	185.00	110.00	195.00	110.00
Salt/Pepper on Tray	145.00	85.00	155.00	110.00	225.00	150.00
Sauce Boat, Underliner	115.00	70.00	165.00	115.00	175.00	125.00
Teacup and Saucer	80.00	40.00	125.00	70.00	135.00	75.00
Teapot, 2-cup	225.00	125.00	350.00	200.00	350.00	200.00
Teapot, 4-cup	350.00	200.00	650.00	325.00	650.00	300.00
Teapot, 6-cup	475.00	300.00	850.00	450.00	950.00	500.00
Teapot, Stacking	600.00	400.00	950.00	525.00	1100.00	575.00
Tennis Set	85.00	50.00	125.00	75.00	145.00	95.00
Toast Rack, 2-slice	150.00	70.00	185.00	105.00	235.00	125.00
Toast Rack, 4-slice	195.00	120.00	235.00	135.00	295.00	155.00
Trivet	75.00	50.00	125.00	80.00	135.00	100.00
Vase, Bud	110.00	50.00	150.00	90.00	175.00	90.00

COMPREHENSIVE PRICE GUIDE FOR CHINTZ

	SPRING		SPRING GLORY		SPRINGTIME	
	U. S. $	U. K. £	U. S. $	U. K. £	U. S. $	U. K. £
Bedside, Breakfast Set	1350.00	650.00	800.00	360.00	800.00	360.00
Bonbon	135.00	95.00	75.00	30.00	75.00	30.00
Bowl, 5"	95.00	45.00	65.00	35.00	65.00	35.00
Butter, Covered	275.00	125.00	225.00	85.00	225.00	85.00
Cake Plate, Open hdl.	225.00	120.00	135.00	85.00	135.00	85.00
Cake Plate, Pedestal	265.00	170.00	140.00	95.00	140.00	95.00
Cake Plate, Tiered	265.00	190.00	150.00	100.00	150.00	100.00
Candy/Sweets Dish	95.00	55.00	65.00	35.00	65.00	35.00
Cheese Keeper, Covd.	300.00	175.00	175.00	115.00	175.00	115.00
Coffee Pot	950.00	600.00	350.00	200.00	350.00	200.00
Compote	225.00	150.00	110.00	65.00	110.00	65.00
Condiment Set on Tray	300.00	185.00	150.00	100.00	150.00	100.00
Creamer and Sugar	135.00	85.00	100.00	60.00	100.00	60.00
Creamer/Sugar on Tray	300.00	95.00	150.00	100.00	150.00	100.00
Demitasse Cup/Saucer	110.00	65.00	75.00	45.00	75.00	45.00
Egg Cup, Footed	100.00	65.00	65.00	30.00	65.00	30.00
Hot Water Jug	500.00	275.00	275.00	150.00	275.00	150.00
Jam Pot w/Underliner	200.00	150.00	125.00	75.00	125.00	75.00
Milk Jug	475.00	250.00	250.00	125.00	250.00	125.00
Pin Tray	95.00	50.00	45.00	25.00	45.00	25.00
Plate, 6"	85.00	45.00	50.00	30.00	50.00	30.00
Plate, 9"	135.00	75.00	60.00	40.00	60.00	40.00
Plate, 10"	195.00	85.00	85.00	60.00	85.00	60.00
Relish	195.00	95.00	125.00	75.00	125.00	75.00
Salad Bowl (Chrome Rim)	195.00	110.00	105.00	60.00	105.00	60.00
Salt/Pepper on Tray	225.00	150.00	150.00	85.00	150.00	85.00
Sauce Boat, Underliner	175.00	125.00	115.00	70.00	115.00	70.00
Teacup and Saucer	135.00	75.00	80.00	45.00	80.00	45.00
Teapot, 2-cup	350.00	200.00	225.00	125.00	225.00	125.00
Teapot, 4-cup	650.00	300.00	350.00	200.00	350.00	200.00
Teapot, 6-cup	950.00	500.00	475.00	300.00	475.00	300.00
Teapot, Stacking	1100.00	575.00	650.00	425.00	650.00	425.00
Tennis Set	145.00	95.00	85.00	50.00	85.00	50.00
Toast Rack, 2-slice	235.00	125.00	125.00	70.00	125.00	70.00
Toast Rack, 4-slice	295.00	155.00	185.00	120.00	185.00	120.00
Trivet	135.00	100.00	75.00	50.00	75.00	50.00
Vase, Bud	175.00	90.00	100.00	60.00	100.00	60.00

COMPREHENSIVE PRICE GUIDE FOR CHINTZ

	STRATFORD		SUMMERTIME		SUNSHINE	
	U. S. $	U. K. £	U. S. $	U. K. £	U. S. $	U. K. £
Bedside, Breakfast Set	800.00	360.00	950.00	600.00	950.00	600.00
Bonbon	75.00	40.00	85.00	45.00	85.00	45.00
Bowl, 5"	65.00	35.00	65.00	40.00	65.00	40.00
Butter, Covered	225.00	85.00	225.00	110.00	225.00	110.00
Cake Plate, Open hdl.	135.00	85.00	165.00	80.00	165.00	80.00
Cake Plate, Pedestal	140.00	95.00	165.00	80.00	165.00	80.00
Cake Plate, Tiered	150.00	100.00	170.00	110.00	170.00	110.00
Candy/Sweets Dish	65.00	35.00	65.00	35.00	65.00	35.00
Cheese Keeper, Covd.	175.00	115.00	275.00	145.00	275.00	145.00
Coffee Pot	350.00	200.00	650.00	450.00	650.00	450.00
Compote	110.00	65.00	140.00	95.00	140.00	95.00
Condiment Set on Tray	150.00	100.00	210.00	150.00	210.00	150.00
Creamer and Sugar	100.00	60.00	85.00	50.00	85.00	50.00
Creamer/Sugar on Tray	150.00	100.00	225.00	140.00	225.00	140.00
Demitasse Cup/Saucer	75.00	45.00	95.00	55.00	95.00	55.00
Egg Cup, Footed	65.00	30.00	85.00	50.00	85.00	50.00
Hot Water Jug	275.00	150.00	395.00	225.00	395.00	225.00
Jam Pot w/Underliner	125.00	75.00	165.00	105.00	165.00	105.00
Milk Jug	250.00	125.00	395.00	200.00	395.00	200.00
Pin Tray	45.00	25.00	95.00	35.00	95.00	35.00
Plate, 6"	50.00	30.00	45.00	35.00	45.00	35.00
Plate, 9"	60.00	40.00	125.00	85.00	125.00	85.00
Plate, 10"	85.00	60.00	135.00	95.00	135.00	95.00
Relish	125.00	75.00	150.00	110.00	150.00	110.00
Salad Bowl (Chrome Rim)	105.00	60.00	155.00	110.00	155.00	110.00
Salt/Pepper on Tray	150.00	85.00	175.00	120.00	175.00	120.00
Sauce Boat, Underliner	115.00	70.00	145.00	115.00	145.00	115.00
Teacup and Saucer	80.00	45.00	135.00	75.00	135.00	75.00
Teapot, 2-cup	225.00	125.00	425.00	275.00	250.00	210.00
Teapot, 4-cup	350.00	200.00	425.00	275.00	425.00	275.00
Teapot, 6-cup	475.00	300.00	750.00	395.00	750.00	395.00
Teapot, Stacking	650.00	425.00	850.00	500.00	850.00	500.00
Tennis Set	85.00	50.00	125.00	70.00	125.00	70.00
Toast Rack, 2-slice	125.00	70.00	155.00	115.00	155.00	115.00
Toast Rack, 4-slice	185.00	120.00	225.00	140.00	225.00	140.00
Trivet	75.00	50.00	100.00	70.00	100.00	70.00
Vase, Bud	100.00	60.00	150.00	95.00	150.00	95.00

COMPREHENSIVE PRICE GUIDE FOR CHINTZ

	SWEET NANCY		SWEET PEA		TARTANS	
	U. S. $	U. K. £	U. S. $	U. K. £	U. S. $	U. K. £
Bedside, Breakfast Set	875.00	360.00	1350.00	650.00	550.00	250.00
Bonbon	85.00	50.00	135.00	95.00	50.00	25.00
Bowl, 5"	65.00	35.00	95.00	45.00	45.00	25.00
Butter, Covered	225.00	85.00	275.00	125.00	225.00	100.00
Cake Plate, Open hdl.	135.00	85.00	225.00	120.00	100.00	60.00
Cake Plate, Pedestal	140.00	95.00	265.00	170.00	110.00	65.00
Cake Plate, Tiered	150.00	100.00	265.00	190.00	125.00	75.00
Candy/Sweets Dish	65.00	35.00	95.00	55.00	45.00	25.00
Cheese Keeper, Covd.	175.00	115.00	300.00	175.00	210.00	110.00
Coffee Pot	350.00	200.00	950.00	600.00	395.00	200.00
Compote	110.00	65.00	225.00	150.00	75.00	45.00
Condiment Set on Tray	150.00	100.00	300.00	185.00	135.00	75.00
Creamer and Sugar	100.00	60.00	135.00	85.00	65.00	40.00
Creamer/Sugar on Tray	150.00	100.00	300.00	95.00	135.00	85.00
Demitasse Cup/Saucer	75.00	45.00	110.00	65.00	55.00	30.00
Egg Cup, Footed	65.00	30.00	100.00	65.00	45.00	25.00
Hot Water Jug	275.00	150.00	500.00	275.00	195.00	110.00
Jam Pot w/Underliner	125.00	75.00	200.00	150.00	95.00	55.00
Milk Jug	250.00	125.00	475.00	250.00	185.00	80.00
Pin Tray	45.00	25.00	95.00	50.00	45.00	25.00
Plate, 6"	50.00	30.00	85.00	45.00	50.00	25.00
Plate, 9"	60.00	40.00	135.00	75.00	75.00	45.00
Plate, 10"	85.00	60.00	195.00	85.00	95.00	50.00
Relish	125.00	75.00	195.00	95.00	95.00	50.00
Salad Bowl (Chrome Rim)	105.00	60.00	195.00	110.00	125.00	65.00
Salt/Pepper on Tray	150.00	85.00	225.00	150.00	100.00	50.00
Sauce Boat, Underliner	115.00	70.00	175.00	125.00	70.00	40.00
Teacup and Saucer	80.00	45.00	135.00	75.00	75.00	30.00
Teapot, 2-cup	225.00	125.00	350.00	200.00	140.00	90.00
Teapot, 4-cup	350.00	200.00	650.00	300.00	225.00	150.00
Teapot, 6-cup	475.00	300.00	950.00	500.00	375.00	210.00
Teapot, Stacking	650.00	425.00	1100.00	575.00	450.00	250.00
Tennis Set	85.00	50.00	145.00	95.00	70.00	40.00
Toast Rack, 2-slice	125.00	70.00	235.00	125.00	110.00	50.00
Toast Rack, 4-slice	185.00	120.00	295.00	155.00	170.00	110.00
Trivet	75.00	50.00	135.00	100.00	50.00	40.00
Vase, Bud	100.00	60.00	175.00	90.00	75.00	40.00

COMPREHENSIVE PRICE GUIDE FOR CHINTZ

	VICTORIAN		VICTORIAN ROSE		VIOLETS	
	U. S. $	U. K. £	U. S. $	U. K. £	U. S. $	U. K. £
Bedside, Breakfast Set	550.00	250.00	900.00	360.00	800.00	360.00
Bonbon	55.00	25.00	75.00	40.00	70.00	35.00
Bowl, 5"	45.00	25.00	65.00	35.00	65.00	35.00
Butter, Covered	225.00	100.00	225.00	85.00	225.00	85.00
Cake Plate, Open hdl.	100.00	60.00	135.00	85.00	135.00	85.00
Cake Plate, Pedestal	110.00	65.00	140.00	95.00	140.00	95.00
Cake Plate, Tiered	125.00	75.00	150.00	100.00	150.00	100.00
Candy/Sweets Dish	45.00	25.00	65.00	35.00	65.00	35.00
Cheese Keeper, Covd.	210.00	110.00	175.00	115.00	175.00	115.00
Coffee Pot	395.00	200.00	350.00	200.00	350.00	200.00
Compote	75.00	45.00	110.00	65.00	110.00	65.00
Condiment Set on Tray	135.00	75.00	150.00	100.00	150.00	100.00
Creamer and Sugar	65.00	40.00	100.00	60.00	100.00	60.00
Creamer/Sugar on Tray	135.00	85.00	150.00	100.00	150.00	100.00
Demitasse Cup/Saucer	55.00	30.00	75.00	45.00	75.00	45.00
Egg Cup, Footed	45.00	25.00	65.00	30.00	65.00	30.00
Hot Water Jug	195.00	110.00	275.00	150.00	275.00	150.00
Jam Pot w/Underliner	95.00	55.00	125.00	75.00	125.00	75.00
Milk Jug	185.00	80.00	250.00	125.00	250.00	125.00
Pin Tray	45.00	25.00	45.00	25.00	45.00	25.00
Plate, 6"	50.00	25.00	50.00	30.00	50.00	30.00
Plate, 9"	75.00	45.00	60.00	40.00	60.00	40.00
Plate, 10"	95.00	50.00	85.00	60.00	85.00	60.00
Relish	95.00	50.00	125.00	75.00	125.00	75.00
Salad Bowl (Chrome Rim)	125.00	65.00	105.00	60.00	105.00	60.00
Salt/Pepper on Tray	100.00	50.00	150.00	85.00	150.00	85.00
Sauce Boat, Underliner	70.00	40.00	115.00	70.00	115.00	70.00
Teacup and Saucer	75.00	30.00	80.00	45.00	80.00	45.00
Teapot, 2-cup	140.00	90.00	225.00	125.00	225.00	125.00
Teapot, 4-cup	225.00	150.00	350.00	200.00	350.00	200.00
Teapot, 6-cup	375.00	210.00	475.00	300.00	475.00	300.00
Teapot, Stacking	450.00	250.00	650.00	425.00	650.00	425.00
Tennis Set	70.00	40.00	85.00	50.00	85.00	50.00
Toast Rack, 2-slice	110.00	50.00	125.00	70.00	125.00	70.00
Toast Rack, 4-slice	175.00	110.00	185.00	120.00	185.00	120.00
Trivet	50.00	40.00	75.00	50.00	75.00	50.00
Vase, Bud	75.00	40.00	100.00	60.00	100.00	60.00

COMPREHENSIVE PRICE GUIDE FOR CHINTZ

	WELBECK		WINIFRED		WHITE ROSE	
	U. S. $	U. K. £	U. S. $	U. K. £	U. S. $	U. K. £
Bedside, Breakfast Set	1500.00	700.00	550.00	250.00	600.00	300.00
Bonbon	125.00	70.00	45.00	20.00	50.00	35.00
Bowl, 5"	95.00	50.00	40.00	25.00	45.00	25.00
Butter, Covered	375.00	210.00	135.00	85.00	125.00	75.00
Cake Plate, Open hdl.	325.00	175.00	90.00	60.00	125.00	75.00
Cake Plate, Pedestal	335.00	210.00	100.00	60.00	125.00	75.00
Cake Plate, Tiered	350.00	215.00	110.00	65.00	135.00	80.00
Candy/Sweets Dish	95.00	50.00	40.00	25.00	35.00	20.00
Cheese Keeper, Covd.	495.00	275.00	145.00	95.00	175.00	105.00
Coffee Pot	1250.00	750.00	375.00	210.00	315.00	195.00
Compote	250.00	140.00	75.00	45.00	85.00	45.00
Condiment Set on Tray	395.00	225.00	125.00	70.00	125.00	60.00
Creamer and Sugar	225.00	110.00	65.00	40.00	95.00	50.00
Creamer/Sugar on Tray	375.00	250.00	100.00	55.00	120.00	80.00
Demitasse Cup/Saucer	135.00	75.00	55.00	30.00	55.00	25.00
Egg Cup, Footed	95.00	60.00	40.00	25.00	45.00	25.00
Hot Water Jug	600.00	300.00	175.00	110.00	195.00	110.00
Jam Pot w/Underliner	295.00	150.00	95.00	60.00	90.00	55.00
Milk Jug	750.00	350.00	165.00	80.00	155.00	95.00
Pin Tray	125.00	60.00	40.00	25.00	45.00	25.00
Plate, 6"	125.00	70.00	45.00	25.00	40.00	20.00
Plate, 9"	195.00	95.00	65.00	45.00	65.00	40.00
Plate, 10"	225.00	110.00	75.00	50.00	85.00	50.00
Relish	275.00	170.00	75.00	55.00	90.00	55.00
Salad Bowl (Chrome Rim)	275.00	175.00	90.00	65.00	95.00	50.00
Salt/Pepper on Tray	285.00	160.00	100.00	70.00	115.00	65.00
Sauce Boat, Underliner	235.00	155.00	65.00	40.00	85.00	60.00
Teacup and Saucer	175.00	95.00	55.00	30.00	65.00	35.00
Teapot, 2-cup	575.00	350.00	150.00	100.00	165.00	85.00
Teapot, 4-cup	850.00	425.00	225.00	150.00	250.00	125.00
Teapot, 6-cup	1250.00	650.00	375.00	210.00	400.00	200.00
Teapot, Stacking	1400.00	700.00	400.00	265.00	500.00	325.00
Tennis Set	165.00	95.00	75.00	35.00	65.00	45.00
Toast Rack, 2-slice	275.00	150.00	95.00	60.00	125.00	70.00
Toast Rack, 4-slice	350.00	210.00	150.00	110.00	150.00	100.00
Trivet	165.00	100.00	50.00	40.00	65.00	40.00
Vase, Bud	225.00	135.00	75.00	40.00	75.00	50.00

COMPREHENSIVE PRICE GUIDE FOR CHINTZ

WILD FLOWERS

	U. S. $	U. K. £
Bedside, Breakfast Set	1100.00	650.00
Bonbon	95.00	60.00
Bowl, 5"	70.00	40.00
Butter, Covered	325.00	125.00
Cake Plate, Open hdl.	200.00	140.00
Cake Plate, Pedestal	210.00	150.00
Cake Plate, Tiered	225.00	155.00
Candy/Sweets Dish	110.00	55.00
Cheese Keeper, Covd.	250.00	175.00
Coffee Pot	850.00	600.00
Compote	175.00	120.00
Condiment Set on Tray	225.00	145.00
Creamer and Sugar	135.00	85.00
Creamer/Sugar on Tray	235.00	145.00
Demitasse Cup/Saucer	110.00	60.00
Egg Cup, Footed	90.00	50.00
Hot Water Jug	465.00	255.00
Jam Pot w/Underliner	195.00	130.00
Milk Jug	450.00	210.00
Pin Tray	85.00	40.00
Plate, 6"	85.00	40.00
Plate, 9"	145.00	75.00
Plate, 10"	169.00	85.00
Relish	185.00	110.00
Salad Bowl (Chrome Rim)	185.00	110.00
Salt/Pepper on Tray	155.00	110.00
Sauce Boat, Underliner	165.00	115.00
Teacup and Saucer	125.00	70.00
Teapot, 2-cup	350.00	200.00
Teapot, 4-cup	650.00	325.00
Teapot, 6-cup	850.00	450.00
Teapot, Stacking	950.00	525.00
Tennis Set	125.00	75.00
Toast Rack, 2-slice	185.00	105.00
Toast Rack, 4-slice	235.00	135.00
Trivet	125.00	80.00
Vase, Bud	150.00	90.00

DESCRIPTION OF COVER

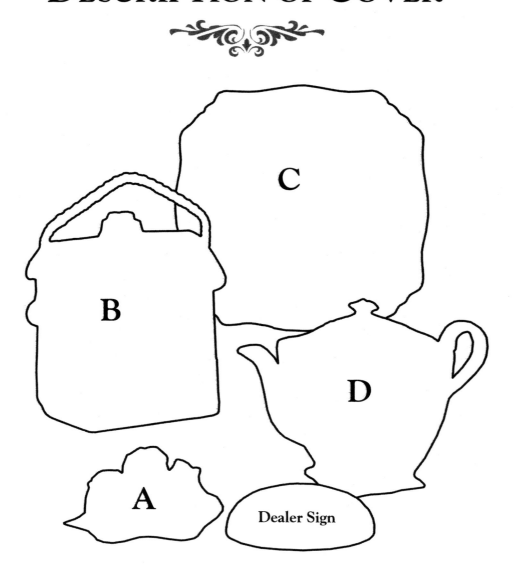

A. Rosebud Condiment Set

B. Cottage Biscuit Barrel

C. Commemorative Plate. This features a WWI cartoon "Coiffure in the Trenches."

D. Summertime Teapot. Courtesy of Cottage Antiques, located on Newport Avenue, San Diego, California.

NOTES

NOTES

NOTES

Notes